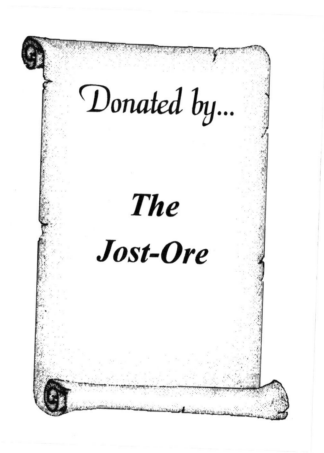

E. F. Jost

Buffalo

11/1/75

"WE FIX 'EM"

The Dern Base Ball Team   1906   Photo By Cros

THAT OLD BALL GAME

rare photographs
from baseball's glorious past

Compiled and Edited by
David R. Phillips
Text by Lawrence Kart

HENRY REGNERY COMPANY • CHICAGO

Library of Congress Cataloging in Publication Data
Main entry under title:

That old ball game.

   1. Baseball—History.   I. Phillips, David R.,
1931-   II. Kart, Lawrence.
GV863.A1T45   1975   796.357'09   75-13240
ISBN 0-8092-8101-1

Copyright © 1975 by David R. Phillips
All rights reserved
Published by Henry Regnery Company
180 North Michigan Avenue, Chicago, Illinois 60601
Manufactured in the United States of America
Library of Congress Catalog Card Number: 75-13240
International Standard Book Number: 0-8092-8401-4

Published simultaneously in Canada by
Fitzhenry & Whiteside Limited
150 Lesmill Road
Don Mills, Ontario M3B 2T5
Canada

Thanks for invaluable assistance to:
Richard Kotnour, Gary George, William Jennings.

A special acknowledgment to the Baseball Hall of Fame,
Cooperstown, New York, and to Francis Burke, whose
photography made this book possible.

To Patrick, Robby, and Pepper

Contents

1
The Early Innings

Activities that involve a stick and a ball have been traced back to pre-Columbian civilizations and even to ancient Egypt, but whether these were games, religious rites, or some other kind of endeavor no one can say. There is little doubt, though, that the immediate ancestor of baseball is rounders—an English game still played by schoolchildren in the British Isles and Australia.

The rules of rounders reveal it to be not much more than a variation of that old favorite, tag. Four stones or posts are arranged a reasonable distance apart in a diamond pattern; the players on hand divide into two sides, one at bat and one in the field; and the feeder delivers the ball to the striker, who hits it and runs the bases as far as he can. The striker is out if he misses the ball three times, if his hit is caught on the fly, or if he is plunked by a thrown ball as he runs the bases. This last aspect of the game seemed to appeal to North America's colonists, and they gave the sport a touch of the rugged frontier by playing with a much harder ball than was normal in the mother country.

Rounders became popular in New England, where it was known as town ball (contests were generally held on Town Meeting Day with all able-bodied hands participating) or burn ball (a reference to the pain endured by a runner who had been put out by a well-aimed throw). The sport was primitive, but this was one of its strengths since the game could easily be shaped to suit the fancy of the players. By 1800, two distinct forms had emerged. The Massachusetts Game had bases set 60 feet apart in an open quadrangle with the striker placed halfway between first and home, a "one out, all out" rule (formerly every man had to be put out before the sides changed), a limit of 14 players per team, and a definite conclusion—the first side to score 100 runs was the winner. The Philadelphia Game was even closer to modern baseball, with the striker standing at the home-base corner of an elongated diamond, a nine-inning

rule instead of the 100-run total to conclude play, and a more genteel way of putting the runner out—either he or the base he was headed for could be tagged with the ball.

In fact, the promotion of gentility was one of Alexander Cartwright's motives when he drew up a list of rules in 1845 for what came to be known as the New York Game. Cartwright was one of a group of young upper-middle class men who had been spending their leisure time playing ball, and he proposed the creation of a social club (akin to a modern country club). To formalize their sport and thus ensure its exclusivity, Cartwright wrote down the way he thought ball should be played. Among his provisions—which were adopted by his fellow members of the Knickerbocker Base Ball Club on September 23, 1845—were the following: "Bases shall be from home to second and first to third, 42 paces equidistant [almost precisely the modern distance]; three men out, all out; the game is to consist of 21 counts or aces [runs], but at the conclusion an equal number of hands [innings] must be played; and a player running the bases shall be out if the ball is in the hands of an adversary on the base and the runner is touched by it, however, in no instance is the ball to be thrown at him."

Cartwright's amalgamation of the Massachusetts and Philadelphia games was an immediate success, and soon his club was meeting other New York-area teams like the Gothams and the Excelsiors in gentlemanly contests under the new rules. But the New York Game could not be restricted to the elite for long, and young workingmen who were not so dedicated as the Knickerbockers to an afternoon of quiet amusement began to play the game with victory as their prime goal, developing such tactics as the bunt, the slide, and the stolen base. Matches between skilled nines aroused intense spectator interest, and a game held in 1858 between picked squads from New York and Brooklyn

The exploits of the 1869 Cincinnati Red Stockings—the first team to admit they were playing for pay—inspired this tune, which could be played as a polka, schottisch, or march. Note the pitcher's underhand delivery—the above-the-belt motion was not allowed until 1884.

drew 1,500 fans (or "cranks" as they were then called) who paid 50 cents apiece for admission to the grounds (a charge levied both to defray expenses and to keep out the rougher element).

By 1858 the game had spread throughout the eastern states, and, in a convention held in New York to draft bylaws and a constitution, the National Association of Base Ball Players was formed ("base ball" would be the standard spelling for some time). Among the changes made in the rules was the replacement of Cartwright's "21-aces" system by the nine-inning game and a prohibition against catching fly balls in one's cap. Two further refinements came in the following decade—a fly caught on one bounce was no longer an out, and the calling of balls and strikes was begun (previously a batter could wait through as many pitches as he wished until one that suited him was delivered).

But important as these rule changes were, the Civil War had an even more profound effect on the evolution of baseball. Vast numbers of young men were brought together, and, in moments of leisure, troops from baseball-playing cities and towns demonstrated the swift, exciting sport. Spectators became participants as they picked up the rules, and those Johnnys fortunate enough to march home after Appamattox included many converts to what some were beginning to call the national game.

In the immediate postwar era, baseball still claimed to be an amateur sport, but this was true in name only. Every club of stature had on its roster strong young "clerks" or "bookkeepers" who were paid ten times the normal wage even though they never stocked a shelf or lifted a ledger. It remained for baseball's Wright brothers to bring things out into the open. The citizens of Cincinnati, annoyed because their local heroes had been trounced in 1867 by the touring Washington Nationals, decided to buy themselves a winning team, and they picked Harry Wright, a British-born cricket instructor who had switched to the American sport, as the man to do the job. They chose wisely, and by the opening of the 1869 season Harry had assembled a powerful squad that featured brother George Wright, the best player of the day, at shortstop. Only one member of the Red Stockings was a Cincinnati native, and salaries for the eight-month season averaged slightly more than $1,000 per man (George earned $1,400, the highest pay). The Red Stockings toured the country, finishing the season without a single defeat. Harry Wright's heroes had caught the nation's fancy, and the future of professional baseball in some form or other was assured as other cities moved to salvage wounded civic pride by organizing their own paid teams.

But the course of professional ball would be far from smooth. Players jumped from one team to another when their salary requests were not met (the Wrights and other Red Stocking stars went to Boston); matches were haphazardly organized and officiated; and heavy betting on games was an open scandal. The National Association of Professional Base Ball Players, formed in 1871, brought a semblance of order to the game, but it was too weak to deal with major abuses. A new kind of organization was needed, and William Hulbert and Albert Spalding set out to provide it.

Hulbert, president of the Chicago club, sought to strengthen his team for the 1876 season by raiding the champion Boston Red Stockings. He contacted Spalding, Boston's star pitcher, who secretly recruited the team's best men, but word of the coup leaked out and Spalding and the others were threatened with expulsion by the National Association. Hulbert quickly realized that the stars he had under contract carried more weight in the baseball world than the Association itself, and he and Spalding proceeded to create their own organization, the National League of Professional Base Ball Clubs, which survives to this day.

Because the National League was run by businessmen instead of ballplayers, it was on stronger economic ground than the National Association, and it was not long before the league's magnates moved to solidify their control with the creation of the reserve rule, which bound athletes to their teams as if they were galley slaves. Hulbert ran the National League with a stern hand until his death in 1882, and by that time it was strong enough to endure the challenge of the American Association, which featured a 25-cent admission charge (half the National League price) and Sunday games.

Meanwhile, important changes in the playing rules had brought baseball even closer to its present-day form. After frequent fluctuations, the number of balls required for a walk was fixed at four and the number of strikes for an out at three. The pitching distance was increased from 45 feet to 50 feet; all restrictions on pitching delivery were eliminated; and the batter was no longer able to call for a low or high pitch. In general, two things had been accomplished—the pitcher, liberated from his role as a mere dispenser of objects to be hit, was now the most specialized and artful man in the game, and a reasonable balance had been struck between offense and defense. Baseball had come a long way from Alexander Cartwright's Knickerbockers, and by 1890 it was a sophisticated, fundamentally sound game that had captured the national interest as both a spectator and a participant sport. Trials and triumphs were yet to come, but baseball was perched confidently on first and looking for ways to advance.

Photographer, Mathew Brady

The myth that Brigadier General Abner Doubleday invented baseball in Cooperstown, N.Y., in 1839 was a piece of pure chauvinism promulgated at the turn of the century in an attempt to deny the game's obviously English origins. Doubleday himself never made any such claim. His uniform, however, is a reminder that the Civil War had a great effect on the spread of the sport. Troops on both sides played the game—40,000 soldiers witnessed a match between two teams from the 165th New York Volunteer Infantry—and after the war they brought baseball to virtually every hamlet in the nation.

Photo. by Brady.

Eng. d by J.C. Buttre.

A. Doubleday

BRIG. GEN. ABNER DOUBLEDAY

Two of baseball's true pioneers were Alexander Cartwright (far left) and Harry Wright (left). Cartwright founded the first notable organized team, the Knickerbocker Baseball Club of New York, in 1845. Even more important was his formulation of the New York Game, which established many of the sport's key rules—in particular, nine men to a side, and equidistant bases 90 feet apart, arranged in a diamond pattern. Wright, shown here as the captain of the Boston Red Stockings, was a professional cricketeer who turned to baseball and created the Cincinnati Red Stockings—the team's distinctive hosiery was visible because Wright chose knickers for their uniforms instead of the customary long pants. Wright, whose team won four straight pennants and a total of six in seven years, did more than anyone else to make professional baseball a legitimate sport.

Photographer, Moffet

Two more of the game's vital early figures—Albert G. Spalding (left) and Henry Chadwick (above). Spalding, a great pitcher (he was 56 and 5 for the Boston Red Stockings in 1875), helped to found the first enduring professional association, the National League, in 1876. Chadwick was a native Englishman who devoted himself to the American sport. He was one of the early sportswriters, a codifier of rules, and baseball's first statistician. Every fan who has spent an evening poring over the records of past seasons owes a debt of gratitude to Father Chadwick.

Old Red Stockings (Cincinnati) 1869
Won all games played season of 1869

1. C. A. McVey
R. F.
2. C. H. Gould
1. B.
3. Harry Wright
Cap. C. F.
4. G. Wright
S. S.
5. F. Waterman
3. B.

6. A. J. Leonard
L. F.
7. D. Allison
C.
8. A. Brainard
P.
9. C. Sweasy
2. B.

The Cincinnati Reds of 1869. Their record that year, in which they toured the country taking on all comers, was 56 victories and 1 tie. Number 1, Calvin McVey, right field; number 2, Charles Gould, first base; number 3, Harry Wright, captain and center field; number 4, George Wright (Harry's brother and the finest all-around player of the day), shortstop; number 5, Fred Waterman, third base; number 6, Andrew Leonard, left field; number 7, Douglas Allison, catcher; number 8, Asa Brainard, pitcher; and number 9, Charles Sweasy, second base. Note the cleats visible on Brainard's shoes.

The popularity of baseball spawned a host of tunes and dances glorifying the game, such as the Home Run Quick Step and the Base Ball Quadrille.

T. J. Foley, 3 b.   R. C. Barnes, s. s.   A. Barker, l. f.   D. Sawyer, c. f.   Fred Cone, 1 b.   R. E. Addy, c.   A. G. Spalding,

FOREST CITY BASE BALL CLU

ROCKFORD,   ILLINOIS.

King, r. f.   Scott Hastings, 2 b.

G. W. BARNES, photographer.

1869.

The 1869 Forest City Base Ball Club of Rockford, Illinois—two years after their 17-year-old pitcher Albert Spalding had startled the baseball world by defeating the supposedly unstoppable Washington Nationals 29 to 23. Although the score suggests that Spalding was not very effective that day, Washington scored 49 runs in their next game against the vaunted Chicago Excelsiors. Another notable member of the squad was shortstop Ross Barnes, who averaged over .400 for three seasons in the 1870s. In the photo, Barnes is second from the left and Spalding is third from the right.

Adrian Constantine "Cap" Anson played first base for the Chicago National League club for 22 years and was their manager for all but the first three of those seasons. Between 1880 and 1886 his White Stockings won five pennants. A stern disciplinarian with a harsh tongue, Anson was one of the power hitters of his era, batting a lusty .395 in 1894 at the age of 43.

Luke Everhard of the Marshalltown, Iowa, team in a uniform that owes its style to the Zouave dress of Civil War volunteer regiments. Marshalltown was Cap Anson's hometown, and when he first broke into organized ball he was known as Baby Anson because he was the first non-Indian born in the hamlet.

The well-dressed man on the field could sport a variety of uniforms in the early days. Note that the dickey was common and usually carried the team insignia.

The ladies in this 1889 print seem more interested in each other's finery than in the progress of play. By the 1880s, female attention had increased, and the first ladies' days were established. They began, according to one story, when the owner of the Cincinnati Reds noticed that feminine attendance was high on the days that handsome Tony Mullane was the pitcher. Thereafter, when Mullane was scheduled to work, women accompanied by escorts were allowed in the park without charge.

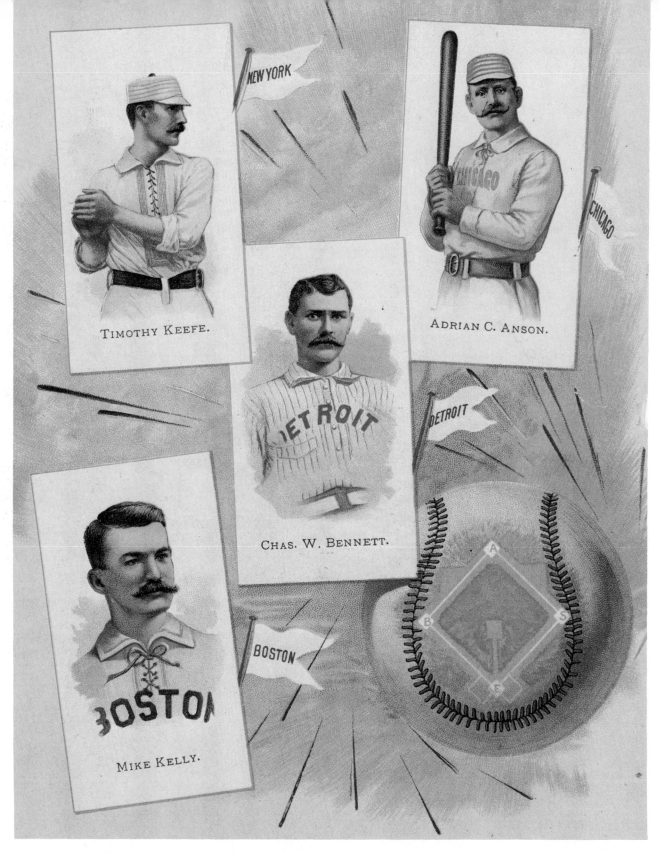

TIMOTHY KEEFE.

ADRIAN C. ANSON.

CHAS. W. BENNETT.

MIKE KELLY.

An early baseball card features National League stars of 1888: Tim Keefe, the legendary New York Giant pitcher who won 19 games in a row that year; Cap Anson of the White Stockings, who led the league with a .344 average; Detroit's Charlie Bennett, one of the best backstops of the day; and Boston's flamboyant King Kelly.

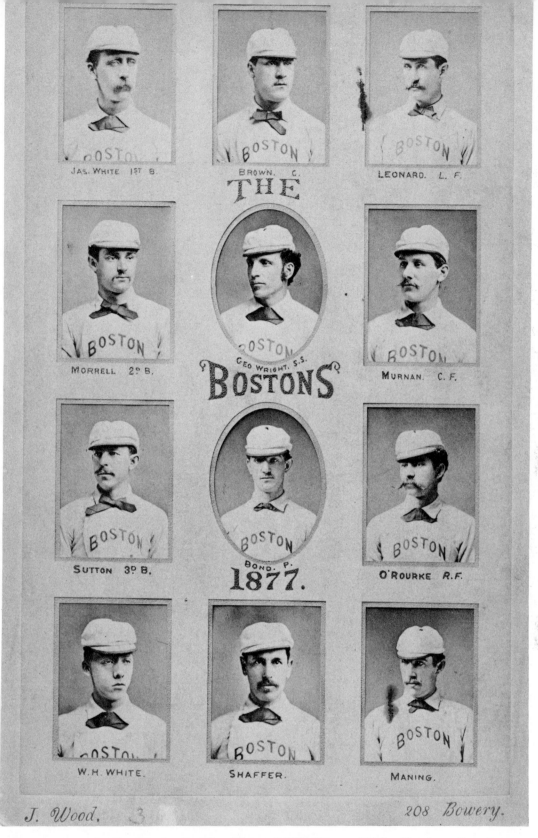

The pennant-winning Boston Red Stockings of 1877: Deacon White, first base; Lew Brown, catcher; Andy Leonard, left field; John Morrill, third base; George Wright, second base; Tim Murnane, center field; Ezra Sutton, shortstop; Tommy Bond, pitcher; Jim "Orator" O'Rourke, right field; Will White, pitcher; Jack Manning, infield. Orator O'Rourke, who earned his nickname with a fountain of rodomontade, caught a full game for the New York Giants in 1904 when he was 52 and went one for four.

Photographer, J. Wood

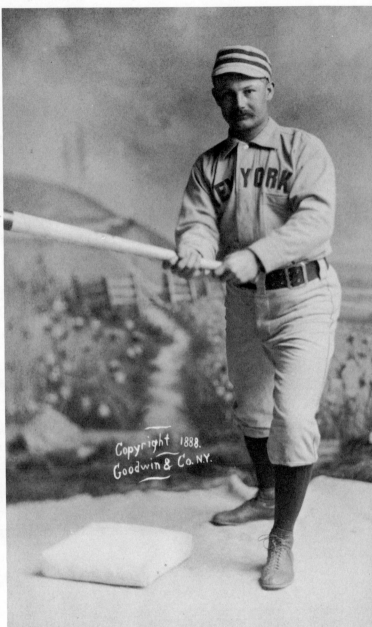

Photographer, Marshall Gilling

Early players often took their uniforms home with them and posed for "action" photos. Players unknown.

Photographer, Anderson Studio   Photographer, Everton Studio

The 1885 St. Louis Browns of the American Association, with player-manager Charlie Comiskey third from the right in the back row. That year he led the Browns to the first of four straight pennants.

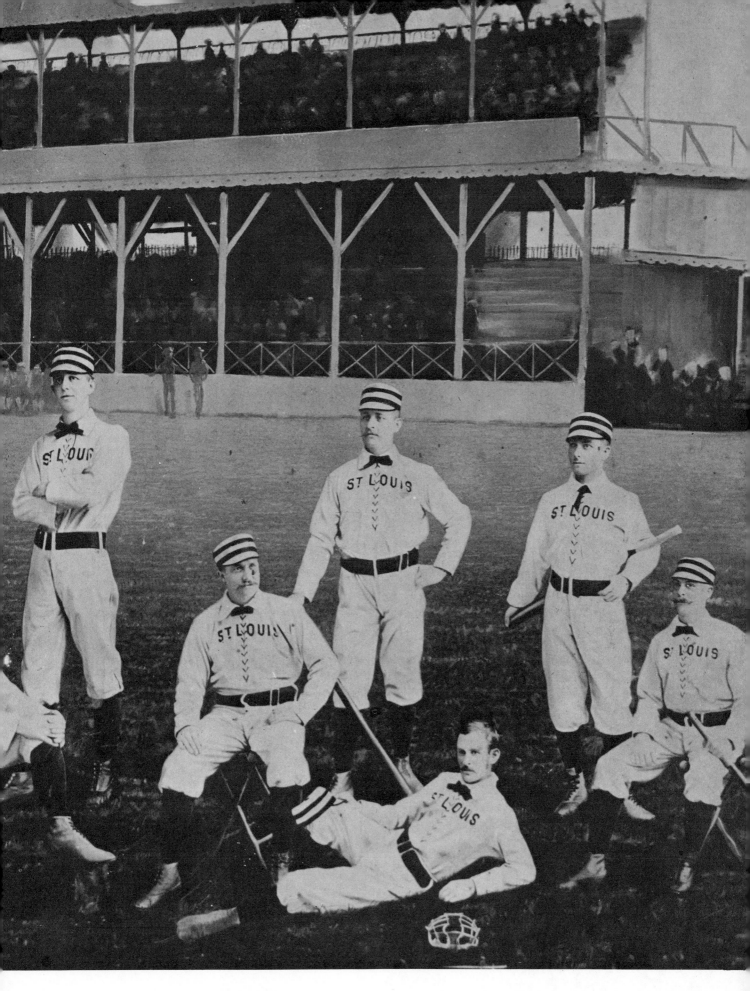

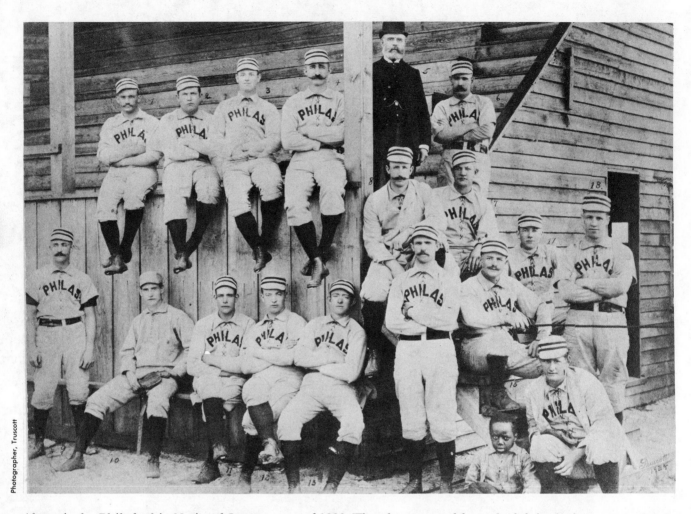

Above is the Philadephia National League team of 1890. The player second from the left in the bottom row has a rather modern-looking catcher's mitt. The Cincinnati Red Stockings (right), champions of the American Association in 1882, met the National League champion Chicago White Stockings in an embryonic World Series that was called off after each team had won a game. Back row (left to right): Harry McCormick, pitcher; Phil Powers, catcher; Dan Stearns, first base; Bid McPhee, second base. Middle row: Hick Carpenter, third base; Pop Snyder, catcher; Will White, pitcher; Chick Fulmer, shortstop; Joe Sommer, left field. Bottom row: Jimmy Macullar, center field; Harry Wheeler, right field. Will White, who had a 40 and 12 record that year, is an interesting figure—he was the first major leaguer to wear eyeglasses on the field, and it is believed that the rule that gives first base to a batter hit by a pitched ball was made necessary by White, who had a penchant for plunking players to drive them back from the plate. Despite his mild-mannered appearance, White's nickname was "Whoop-la"—perhaps the monicker was bestowed ironically.

CINCINNATIS.
CHAMPIONS 1882.
AMERICAN ASSOCIATION.

McCormick—P.		Deyers—C.		Stearns—1st B.		McPhee—2d B.
Carpenter—3d B.	Snyder—C.	White—P.	Fulmer—S. S.	Sommer—L. F.
	Macullar—C. F.		Wheeler—R. F.	

Photographer, Landy

1. Ryan.
2. Williamson.
3. Farrell.
4. Pfeffer.
5. The Mascot.

JOS. HALL, Photo., Brooklyn, N. Y.

6. Capt. Anson.
7. Van Haltren.
8. Borchers.
9. Burns.
10. Daly.

CHICAGO BALL CLUB, 1888.

The 1888 Chicago White Stockings, second place team in the National League: 1, Jimmy Ryan, outfield; 2, Ned Williamson, shortstop; 3, Duke Farrell, catcher-outfield; 4, Fred Pfeffer, second base; 5, Clarence Duvall, mascot; 6, Cap Anson, first base-manager; 7, George Van Haltren, outfield; 8, George Borchers, pitcher; 9, Tom Burns, third base; and 10, Tom Daly, catcher. The proximity of Duvall and Anson is interesting since Cap, a violently prejudiced man, was more responsible than any other figure for the barring of black Americans from professional baseball.

Photographer, Jos. Hall

Louisville Ball Club, 1888.

The 1887 Louisville club of the American Association, a major league from 1882 to 1891. Lower row (left to right): Toad Ramsey, pitcher; Icebox Chamberlain, pitcher; Bill White, shortstop; Honest John Kelly, manager; Scott Stratton, outfield-pitcher; Chicken Wolf, outfield; and Hub Collins, outfield. Upper row: Skyrocket Smith, first base; Guy Hecker, pitcher-first base; Pete Browning, outfield; John Kerins, outfield; Paul Cook, catcher; and Joe Werrick, third base. Louisville may have finished seventh that season, but with Ramsey, Chamberlain, Wolf and Smith they certainly led the league in nicknames. Kelly, their manager, was a celebrated umpire in prior years.

Photographer, Jos. Hall

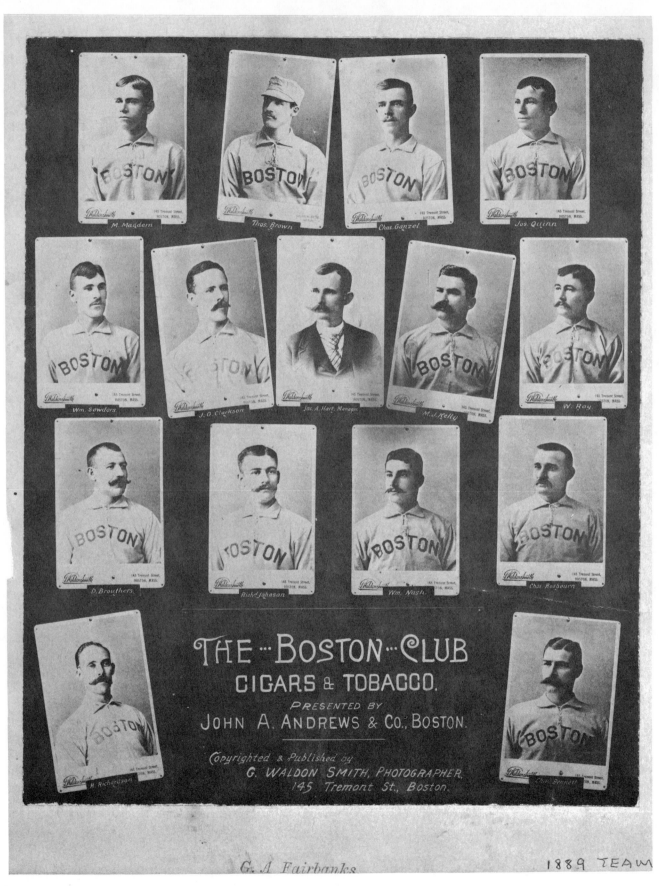

Photographer, G. Waldon Smith

The 1889 Boston Red Stockings on an early baseball card. Top row (left to right): Kid Madden, pitcher; Tom Brown, outfield; Charlie Ganzel, catcher; Joe Quinn, shortstop; Second row: Bill Sowders, pitcher; John Clarkson, pitcher; Jim Hart, manager; King Kelly, outfield; Irv Ray, shortstop. Third row: Dan Brouthers, first base; Dick Johnston, outfield; Billy Nash, third base; Old Hoss Radbourn, pitcher. Bottom row: Hardy Richardson, second base; and Charlie Bennett, catcher. There are four Hall of Fame members on this team—Clarkson (who won 49 games that year); Kelly of "Slide, Kelly, Slide" (the most colorful player of the era); Brouthers, the holder of a .342 lifetime batting average; and Radbourn, who pitched 36 of the last 39 games for Providence in 1884, including 22 in a row. Above are the Red Stockings of 1890, a year when most of the top players had defected to the idealistic Players League.

Photographer, W. Phillippi

Charles A. Comiskey looking quite natty during his tenure as player-manager of the American Association St. Louis Browns.

Photographer, Fischer Studio

Comiskey, who helped organize the American League and became the manager and owner of the Chicago White Sox, was the founder of modern first base play, letting the pitcher cover the bag as he raced far into right field to flag down hot grounders.

The Bloomington, Illinois, Reds of 1888, a minor league team. Second from the left in the back row is the 18-year-old Clark Griffith, a fine pitcher for the Chicago White Stockings in the 1890s, who became the manager and president of the Washington Senators. His canny player trades earned him his nickname, "The Old Fox."

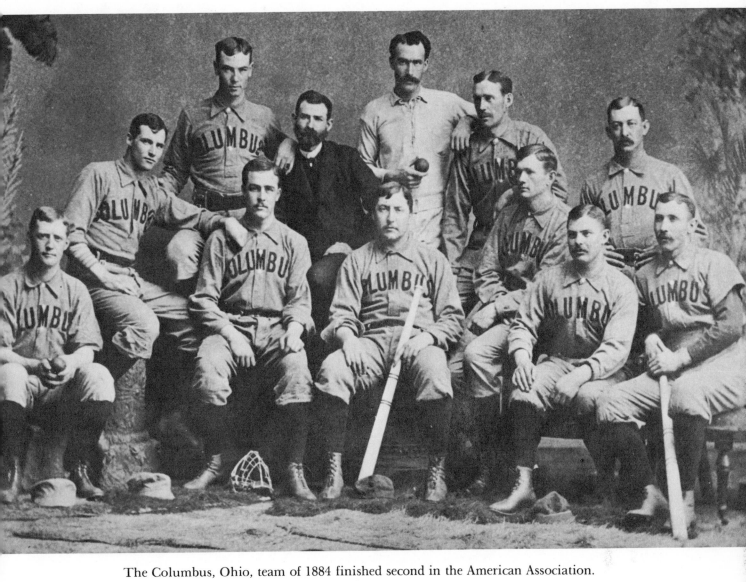

The Columbus, Ohio, team of 1884 finished second in the American Association.

An unknown southpaw (left) and Hall of Fame shortstop Joe Tinker in his early days as a member of the Galena, Illinois, semi-pro club.

Photographer, Winsor Studio

Photographer, Hardy/Van Arnam Studio

Two more unidentified players posing for the studio photographer. The man on the left played for the team of Cooperstown, New York, where, considering the quilted uniform, it must have been nippy early in the season. The other fellow was a catcher for Troy, New York. Note his mask and small glove—bravery has always been a prerequisite for a backstop.

The Ithaca, New York, team of 1874 and 1875 adopted some atypical headgear.

The 1877 Star's team, city unknown.

The famous evangelist Billy Sunday, an outfielder (left) for Chicago and Pittsburgh from 1883 to 1890, appealed to the Lord to help him catch fly balls. Since Billy was perhaps the fastest man in the game, his prayers were often answered, but Jesus apparently frowned on offense—Sunday's lifetime batting average was only .248. It was as a purveyor of salvation (right) that Billy made his mark, and from 1896 (when he hit the sawdust circuit) to his death in 1935 he was unrivaled as a decrier of sinfulness, often drawing on his baseball experience to make his points.

Photographer, Francis P. Burke

Photographer, Francis P. Burke

37

2

The Awkward Years

The years from 1890 to 1910 mark baseball's adolescence, and the era began characteristically with an outburst of rebellion. The National League club owners, having stripped the players of any control over their own destinies with the reserve rule, now imposed an upper limit on salaries and, most infuriating of all, a classification system in which pay was based on decorum, dedication, character, and other owner-adjudged niceties. This was more than the players could stand, and their organization, the Brotherhood of Professional Baseball Players, made plans to retaliate. Led by John Montgomery Ward—the New York Giants' shortstop who had a law degree from Columbia University—they considered a strike but then adopted the more radical idea of establishing their own major league in time for the 1890 season. They were certain that most players would join the new league, and the National League would be hard put to attract customers with teams of incompetent scrubs. Financial backing for the Players League was obtained from men like Albert Johnson, the owner of a Cleveland streetcar line who hoped that a ballpark along his route would attract new business, and opening day found three major leagues in existence—the National League, the Players League, and the American Association.

The war among the leagues was a fierce one. Most of the game's stars did join the Players League, which outdrew both competing circuits, but no one made a profit, and the wealthier National League proved better able to withstand adversity. Some of the players' businessmen allies sold out to the National League in a post-season peace conference, and the American Association had been so weakened by the struggle that it gave up the ghost after only one more season.

The players' revolt failed for a number of reasons (prominent among them being individual greed and insufficient capital), but perhaps the most important factor was the attitude of the fans—broad public support for the athletes' grievances could not be obtained so long as the fans looked on baseball as a mere game, and if the fans recognized baseball as the business it was, then their taste for the sport diminished.

During this era, storm and strife invaded the field, too, and the last traces of baseball's genteel past vanished in a welter of bumping, spiking, and umpire-baiting. A win-at-all-costs attitude prevailed, and players used their wits to squeeze the maximum advantage out of every situation. The sharpest, most notorious squad of the 1890s was the Baltimore Orioles, led by their scrappy third baseman John McGraw and their manager Ned Hanlon. The Orioles hid baseballs in the outfield grass for use when long drives eluded them, flashed sunlight into the eyes of enemy batters and fielders with pocket mirrors, banked baselines to favor their bunting, and slipped mushy balls into the game when the other team was at bat.

But other, more legitimate tactical innovations were introduced—among them the development of coordinated defense. Outfielders aimed their throws at cutoff men to trap overly ambitious runners, and infielders positioned themselves around the diamond to meet changing situations—third basemen dashing toward the plate to make bare-handed pickups of bunts, second basemen and shortstops signaling coverage on attempted steals and refining the pivot move for double plays.

The trend toward specialization also affected the offense. The hit-and-run play was perfected, and managers arranged their lineups so that each man had a clearly defined role. The ideal lead-off man was a pesky hitter and fast runner whose job was to get on base by any means possible (a walk or a pitch in the ribs was as good as a hit); the second batter (also a fast man to avoid double plays) was a hit-and-run artist who could place the ball behind the runner; the third-place hitter had the highest batting average; and the clean-up man was a slugger.

38

In later years, Cap Anson, now respectfully called "Pop," threw out the first ball of the season for the Chicago Cubs. Pop's White Stockings became known as the Cubs during the 1901 season after player raids by the new American League had forced Chicago's National League entry to field a young, inexperienced team.

Key changes in the rules also brought the game closer to its present form. The most important of these was the increase in the distance between the pitcher and home plate from 50 feet to 60 feet, 6 inches. Batting averages soared for several seasons until hurlers learned how to adjust their deliveries, but the change was a wise one—it is frightening to imagine what a Walter Johnson fastball would have looked like if it had been launched from a spot ten feet closer to the batter. Foul balls were counted as strikes up to strike two in order to discourage the practice of fouling off an endless number of pitches; a foul bunt on two strikes was an out; and free substitution of players was allowed, with the player removed not being able to re-enter the game (in the past, substitutions could be made only by permission of the opposing team or in case of an injury).

After the failure of the Players League and the demise of the American Association, the National League grew to twelve clubs by absorbing the Association's four healthiest franchises. The resulting structure, however, was unwieldy and unbalanced (Boston and Baltimore won every pennant but one from 1892 to 1899), and two Cincinnati men, sportswriter Ban Johnson and Reds' manager Charles Comiskey, felt that eventually the time would be ripe for the formation of another major league. They acquired control of a minor league with solid midwestern markets and carefully began to strengthen its economic base and raise the level of play. When the National League made several key mistakes after the 1900 season—rejecting peace overtures from Johnson and snubbing demands from the players association—the new American League declared war and began signing National League stars. Johnson's leadership was clever and resourceful, and after the 1902 season in which the American League outdrew the senior circuit, the National League owners saw they were licked and signed a peace agreement that gave the American League equal status.

Now that baseball had two healthy major leagues, it seemed only logical that their respective champions should meet in a post-season series to determine the world title. Such competitions were not new to the game—there had been hotly contested battles between the National League and American Association titlists in the 1880s—but the concept had foundered in the 1890s with the Temple Cup matches, which were lackadaisical affairs between the National League's champion and runner-up. Now, however, with the natural rivalry between leagues stirring fan interest, the Boston Red Sox met the Pittsburgh Pirates in the first modern World Series. The American League's Red Sox won the best-five-out-of-nine series in eight games, and although John McGraw sabotaged the 1904 series by refusing to allow his New York Giants to meet the "upstarts" from the new league, the contests resumed the following year and have continued without a break to this day. An era that had begun with labor strife that threatened to destroy professional baseball was ending with the two major leagues we know today in vigorous existence and with the playing rules in their basic modern form. Baseball's adolescence was over—its adulthood was beginning.

The Baltimore Orioles were one of baseball's strongest clubs in the Gay Nineties, winning pennants in 1894, 1895, and 1896. John McGraw was their leader on the field, a feisty little third baseman with a win-at-all-costs attitude. McGraw was adept at bumping and tripping base runners, and his favorite trick was to slip his fingers inside the belt of a man about to tag up on a fly ball, often delaying the runner just long enough to turn a run into a putout at the plate. Big Ed Delahanty of Philadelphia ended that bit of gamesmanship one day by undoing his buckle as he stood on third. When McGraw grabbed Delahanty's belt, he was left holding the goods while the game's single umpire turned to take in the situation. McGraw and umpires were not on good terms, to say the least, and his violent harassment of arbiters and opposing players made the Orioles an object of hatred in every town in the league but Baltimore. The acquisition of left fielder Joe Kelly from Pittsburgh at the end of the 1892 season was a key move in the transformation of the Orioles from tailenders to champions. From 1894 to 1897 he never hit less than .364, averaged 116 RBI per season, and stole 231 bases. Shortstop Hughie Jennings, just as clever and scrappy as McGraw, was a self-made ballplayer who worked on his faults and became a fine hitter, batting .401 in 1896. He was a master at the painful art of getting a free ride to first by putting his body in the way of a pitched ball. Wee Willie Keeler (5′ 4″, 140 lbs.) was one of the few soft-spoken Orioles and the greatest place hitter in the history of the game. Gripping his bat almost halfway up the handle, he wielded it with surgical precision, dropping hits just over the infielders' heads. He is credited with inventing, or at least perfecting, the "Baltimore Chop"—a sharp downward swing that bounced the ball over a baseman who had charged in expecting a bunt. Wee Willie holds the fifth highest lifetime batting average at .345, and he hit .432 in 1897.

McGRAW.

KELLY.

JENNINGS.

KEELER.

Photographer, Betz

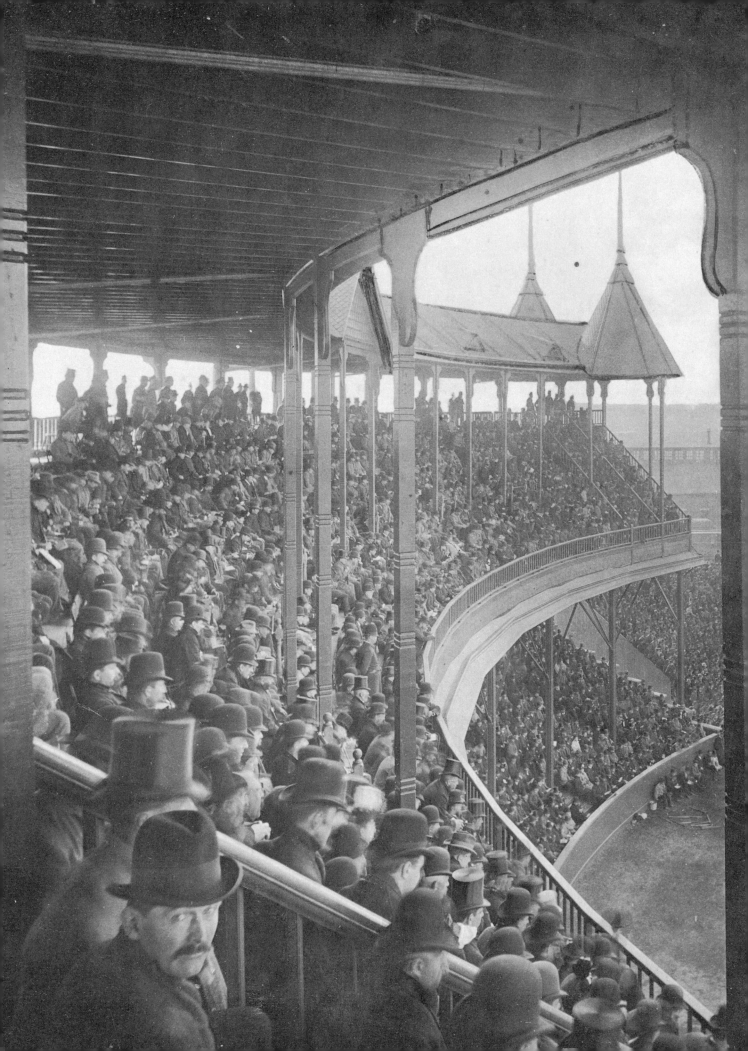

The Grand Pavilion of the Boston Stadium in the 1890s. The Beaneaters were the other strong National League team of the decade—every pennant that Baltimore didn't win between 1891 and 1898 was claimed by the Boston squad. Led by their great manager Frank Selee, the Beaneaters played an artful brand of ball based on pitching and defense. Their infield, anchored at third by Jimmy Collins (the man who perfected the barehand pickup of the bunt) and at first by Tommy Tucker and later Fred Tenney, was also strong through the middle, with the graceful Herman Long at shortstop and Bobby Lowe at second. Kid Nichols was Boston's golden arm—between 1891 and 1897 he never had less than 30 wins a season, completing all but 20 of the 315 games in which he was the starting pitcher. The Bostons were no slouches on offense either, not with outfielders Billy Hamilton and Hugh Duffy at the plate. Sliding Billy was the greatest base thief of the day, and in his first two seasons with the club he stole successfully 215 times. Duffy holds the highest single-season batting average of the modern era, .438 in 1894, but that mark was probably affected by the change of the pitching distance in 1893 from 50 feet to 60 feet, 6 inches—most pitchers needed at least a year to adjust to the longer throw.

Photographer, A.H. Folsom

Rochester team Eastern League 1897.
Transferred to Ottawa Canada.

The 1897 Rochester team of the Eastern League (above) was shifted during the season to Ottawa, Ontario (right) where they were outfitted in highland plaid and accompanied by bagpipers. Joe Gunson (bottom row, second from the right on the Ottawa club) is an example of a journeyman ballplayer on his way down—he had a brief stretch in the majors as a catcher in the early 1890s.

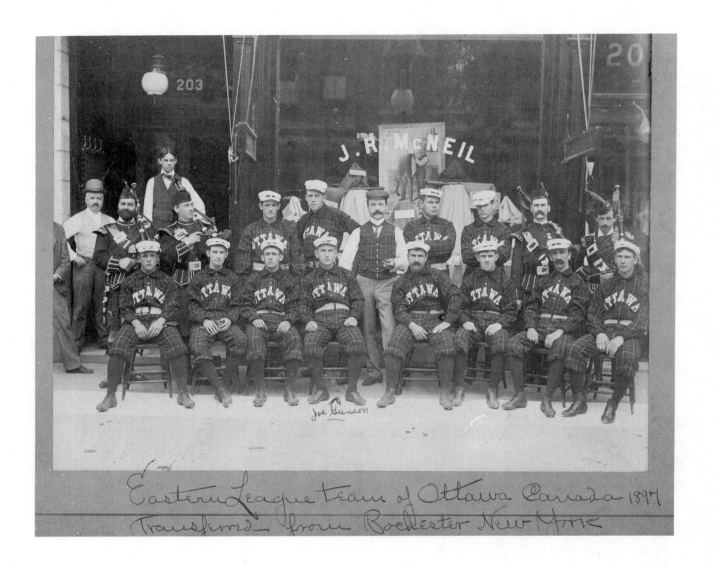

Eastern League team of Ottawa Canada 1897
Transferred from Rochester New York

The Winning Game
Boston vs Balti

Boston finished two games ahead of Baltimore in 1897 and then met the Orioles in a post-season series for the Temple Cup, losing four games to one. This photo shows the standing-room-only crowd that gathered for the deciding game of the regular season. The Cup contests didn't draw nearly as well—most fans (and some of the players) feeling that the issue had already been decided—and the series, which had been marked by controversy in its four years of existence, was discontinued. Interest in post-season play revived in 1903 when the champions of the National and American Leagues met in the first World Series.

Pittsburgh's Honus Wagner, the greatest shortstop of baseball's first half-century, has been nominated by many as the best player of all time. Wagner excelled in every aspect of the game—fielding, throwing, hitting for average and power, base stealing, all-around speed, and strategic sense. In addition, he was a modest man of gentle, even disposition who would rarely complain about an umpire's call or criticize another ballplayer. Note in the photo below one of Wagner's physical assets—his huge hands that enabled him to scoop up grounders like a steam shovel.

Photographer, Francis P. Burke

Wagner heads for first after rifling a shot to the outfield. The Flying Dutchman led the National League in batting eight times and hit over .300 for seventeen consecutive seasons.

Photographer, Francis P. Burke

Wagner warms up in front of an injunction against the placement of a friendly wager. The specter of gambling and fixed games had long haunted baseball, and the Black Sox scandal of 1919 was only the most sensational such incident. One of the reasons the Temple Cup series of the 1890s had failed was that many players agreed to pool their winnings from what was supposed to be a winner-take-all event. When word of this leaked to the public, they assumed quite logically that the games would hardly be exhibitions of competitive zeal.

Photographer, Francis P. Burke

53

Ty Cobb of the Detroit Tigers, the greatest hitter and base stealer of all time, was a man possessed by a demon that drove him to excellence. Any skills he didn't come by naturally were honed to perfection by hours of practice. Although other players respected Cobb's ability, he was one of the most hated men in the game because his fierce will to win, tolerable enough on the field, extended to all aspects of life. In his early days, he fought with his own team-mates, convinced they were against him, and once in the minors he attacked his roomie, pitcher Nap Rucker, for beating him to the bathtub. His words on that occasion could serve as his epitaph—"I gotta be first . . . all the time." Cobb's records include most lifetime hits, runs, and stolen bases, and the highest lifetime batting average (.367), but these marks tell only part of the story. When he was on base he took total control of the game, driving the pitcher and fielders to distraction. A power hitter like Babe Ruth might be able to do more damage more quickly, but Cobb's successes had an edge of humiliation to them. He was not only hated; he was feared. On the left Cobb poses in a bunting stance, while in the superb action shot above he slices the corner of the plate with his patented hook slide, demonstrating in the intensity of his body line and facial expression the determination with which he played the game.

Photographer, Francis P. Burke

Frank Chance, The Peerless Leader, earned his nickname by piloting the Chicago Cubs to four National League championships and two world titles from 1906 to 1910. His 1906 club holds the record for most victories in a season—106. A big man (his other monicker was "Husk" for husky), Chance joined the Cubs in 1898 as a catcher but was converted into a first baseman by manager Frank Selee and soon became a fine fielder at that position. Although he was a strong hitter, Chance, unfortunately, was one of those players who froze at the plate when a ball was thrown at his head. Beaned quite often, he suffered from severe headaches that led to his early death in 1924 at the age of 47.

Photographer, Francis P. Burke

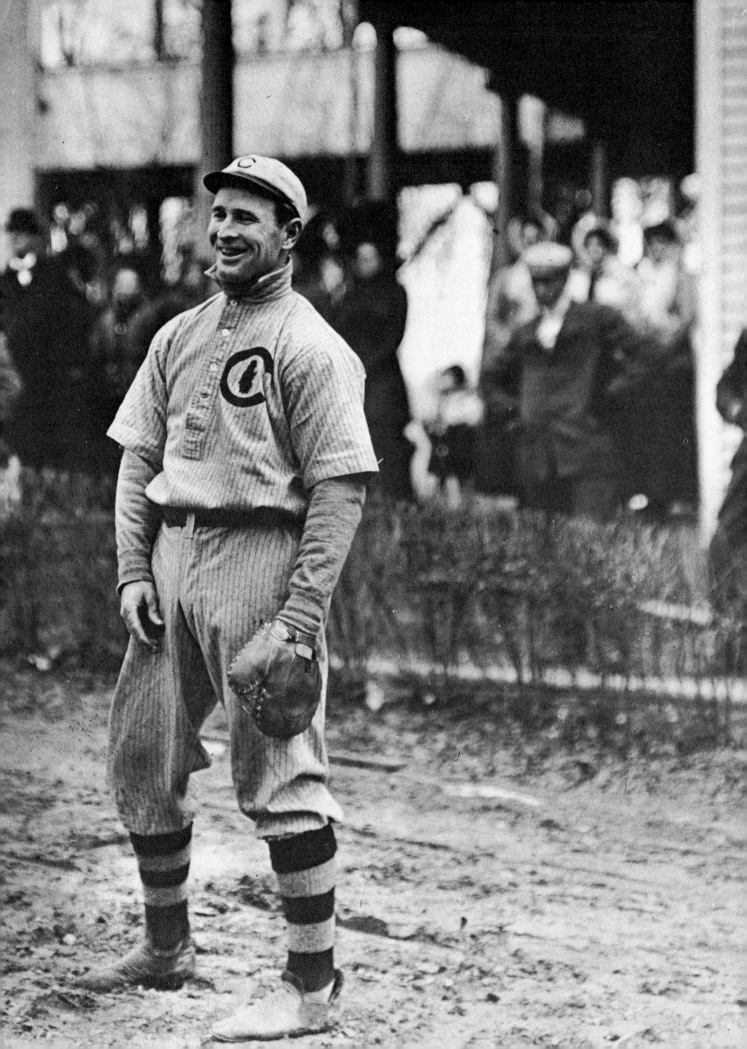

A member of the Philadelphia Athletics scores against the Cubs in the 1910 World Series. Led by their pitching star Jack Coombs, who hurled three complete-game victories, and their heavy hitters, Home Run Baker, Eddie Collins, and Danny Murphy, the Athletics took the Cubs four games to one.

Photographer, Francis P. Burke

58

A logical candidate for the greatest manager of all time would be John McGraw, the man who virtually created the New York Giants. When he took over the helm in 1902, the Giants were a weak club—when he stepped down after the 1932 season, he had piloted the Giants to ten pennants (including four straight from 1921 to 1924) and three world championships, finishing out of the first division only three times in his career. McGraw's nickname, Little Napoleon, accurately described his dictatorial manner. He once fined a player who hit a home run to win a ball game—McGraw had signaled for a bunt, and orders were orders. Muggsy (his other nickname and one that no one dared use to his face) demanded maximum effort from his players at all times, was a fine developer of talent and a master strategist. His influence on baseball was vast and continues to this day—some of the game's finest managers, who in turn influenced others, were schooled by McGraw, and his world tours with the Giants helped make baseball an international game.

Photographer, Francis P. Burke

At the age of seven, Mordecai Peter Centennial Brown mangled his right hand in a corn chopper, losing most of the index finger. When young Mordecai began throwing a baseball several years later, he discovered that his odd grip gave him a natural sinker that also swooped from side to side like a knuckleball. As Three-Finger Brown, he was the Chicago Cubs best moundsman during the Frank Chance era and was especially effective in crucial games. He holds the third-lowest lifetime earned run average and was as fine a fielder as he was a pitcher—with Brown on the hill and Tinker and Evers behind him, there was no way for a ground ball to get through the middle of the Chicago infield.

Rube Oldring was a steady outfielder for the Philadelphia Athletics from 1906 to 1918, playing on four pennant winners and two world champions. Oldring's excuse for his poor play in the 1914 World Series—in which Boston's ''Miracle'' Braves swept the vaunted A's in four games—was worthy of Ring Lardner's Alibi Ike. He was harassed throughout the series, Rube said, by a woman who claimed falsely to be his wife.

Photographer, Francis P. Burke

Photographer, Francis P. Burke

Pitchers Nick Altrock (left) and Rube Waddell (right)—two of baseball's premier eccentrics—helped establish the tradition that all southpaws are flaky. Altrock, who had some good years with the White Sox, was more calculated in his antics than Waddell and earned his principal fame as an outright baseball clown when he and Al Schacht were coaches for the Washington Senators. Waddell, however, was both a great pitcher and a genuine screwball whose vagaries, since they shortened his brilliant career, had more than a touch of pathos to them. Rube was nothing but an overgrown boy who loved to chase fire engines, catch fish, and tend bar as much as he enjoyed setting strikeout records (his total of 349 whiffs in 1904 was the longest standing baseball record—broken only in 1965 by Sandy Koufax and then again in 1973 by Nolan Ryan). Waddell had very little conception of what it meant to be a professional and he didn't hesitate to leave the team for a day or a week if the mood took him. Once at game time on a day he was scheduled to pitch, Rube was found fogging them past a team of kids on a local sandlot. Connie Mack, the gentlest man in baseball, was the only manager who had any success in handling him, and finally even Mack's patience wore thin and Rube was sold to the St. Louis Browns. He had one more good year but contracted pneumonia while serving as a volunteer in a flood. Weakened by this illness, he developed tuberculosis and died in 1914 at the age of 37.

Photographer, Francis P. Burke

CHAS. A. COMISKEY, CHICAGO

JAMES McALEER, BOSTON

BEN SHIBE, PHILA.

A group of varying backgrounds and fortunes—American League club owners circa 1905, surrounding league president Ban Johnson. Farrell was a bookmaker and owned a gambling house; Somers, a coal company heir who provided the league with much of its initial capital, eventually went bankrupt, while Hedges reaped a considerable profit from the Browns.

Photographer, Burke/Atwell

66

FRANK FARRELL, NEW YORK

FRANK NAVIN, DETROIT

BAN JOHNSON
PRES. OF THE AMERICAN LEAGUE

CHAS. SOMERS, CLEVELAND

Photo ©
Burke & Atwell
Chicago

ROBT. L. HEDGES, ST. LOUIS

E. S. MINOR, WASHINGTON

Byron Bancroft Johnson was a young Cincinnati news-paperman in 1893 when he and Charles Comiskey, manager of the Cincinnati Reds, formulated a plan to create a second major league. They revived the Western League—a dormant minor league circuit that included such solid baseball cities as Minneapolis, Milwaukee, Kansas City, and Toledo—and gradually raised the level of play, biding their time until 1900 when the National League sloughed off a request from Johnson to discuss the now-renamed American League's status. Realizing that many National League players were prepared to break their contracts because the owners had turned down some modest requests from the Players Protective Association, Johnson declared war and acquired a number of the senior circuit's stars. By 1902 the American League was outdrawing the opposition, and the following year a peace agreement was signed that ended the bidding contest and made the American League the National's full-fledged equal.

Photographer, Francis P. Burke

Johnson (right center, with National League President John K. Tener, left center) was the undisputed dictator of the American League until the mid-1920s. In one of his most important edicts, he granted umpires absolute authority to keep order on the field. Harassment of the men in blue had become so severe that many felt the very existence of baseball was threatened, but Johnson gave his umpires total support. The combative John McGraw found this restriction frustrating, and after a year and a half of fines from Johnson for umpire-baiting, he left his job as manager of the Baltimore American League club and took over the New York Giants in the National League.

Photographer, Francis P. Burke

70

Photographer, Francis P. Burke

CHICAGO CUBS
NATIONAL LEAGUE CHAMPIONS
1907

Photographer, Francis P. Burke

Top Row	SCHULTE	ZIMMERMAN	REULBACH	LUNDGREN	PEEISTER	HOWARD	OTIS	FRAZER	
Middle Row	TINKER	KLING	SHECKARD	McCORMICK	CHANCE mgr.	STEINFELDT	HOFMAN	OVERALL	MORAN
Bottom Row		DURBIN	BROWN		SLAGLE		EVERS		

Charles Murphy (left), owner of the Chicago Cubs from 1905 to 1914, looks pleased as punch to be in control of the team, but the fans, his players, and fellow executives hardly shared Charlie's view of the situation. Murphy, an ex-newspaperman given to wild charges and sentimental outbursts, was despised by the other club owners, and when he disposed of three of Chicago's heros—Frank Chance, Johnny Evers, and Ed Reulbach—the baseball-loving population of the city was outraged. The National League owners, involved in a difficult struggle with the new Federal League, could ill afford such antics in one of their key markets, and Murphy was forced to sell his share in the team. The 1907 Cubs (above) were one of the squads that made Murphy rich if not popular. They won the pennant by 17 games and took 4 straight from the Detroit Tigers in the World Series.

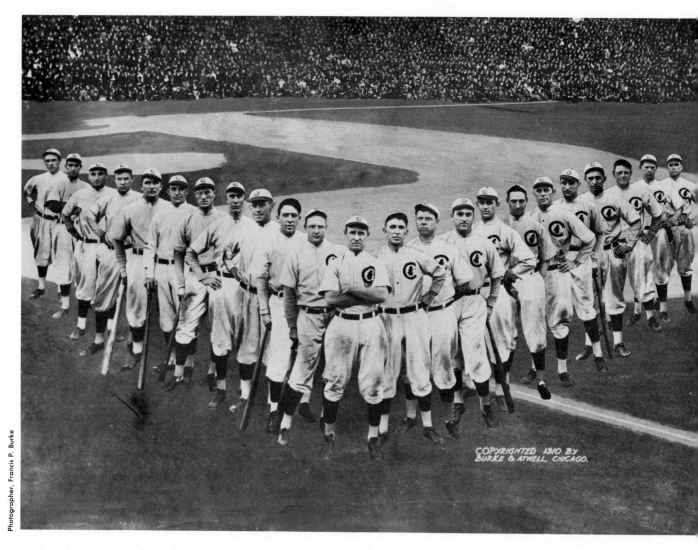

Photographer, Francis P. Burke

The 1910 Cubs (above) and the 1910 Athletics (right) easily won their respective league titles. The Chicago club was heavily favored in the World Series—this was their fourth pennant in five years—but the A's, led by their great manager Connie Mack (pictured here in the center of the Philadelphia squad), were beginning an identical string of their own, and they polished off Chicago in five games. The Cubs would not win another pennant until 1918.

Hughie Jennings, John McGraw's teammate on the old Baltimore Orioles, managed the Detroit Tigers for 14 years, winning three consecutive American League titles from 1907 to 1909. Jennings' nickname, "Eee-yah," came from his antics in the coaching box where he would dance on one leg and bray like a mule in moments of triumph. Hughie, however, was far from a clown—a keen tactician and a gifted handler of men, he was able to get the most out of the turbulent Ty Cobb by simply giving him free rein. Jennings probably understood Cobb's violent nature better than most, since he himself had been a fierce competitor in his playing days.

Photographer, Francis P. Burke

Jennings and Frank Chance of the Cubs chat before a
World Series game. The Tigers and Cubs met for the
world title in 1907 and 1908 with the National League
club winning easily both times.

Photographer, Francis P. Burke

Cubs manager Frank Chance listens
grimly to umpire Rigler lay down the law
in a 1910 World Series Game.

Photographer, Francis P. Burke

Photographer, Francis P. Burke

80

Hank O'Day, a journeyman pitcher in the 1880s, became one of the game's finest umpires, and it was he who made the most controversial ruling in the history of baseball. Near the end of the 1908 season, the Giants faced the Cubs in a game that could clinch the pennant for the New York team. With the score tied one to one, two out in the bottom of the ninth and Giants on first and third, the batter hit a solid shot to center. Moose McCormick trotted across the plate, and the game and the pennant race seemed to be over. But Johnny Evers, the Cubs' second baseman, saw that the runner on first, a 19-year-old rookie named Fred Merkle, had advanced only halfway to second and then turned to the clubhouse to avoid the crowd surging onto the field. The wily Evers, who knew that if the last out of an inning is a force-out no runs can score on that play, screamed to the center fielder to throw him the ball. Here accounts become unclear, but apparently Iron Man McGinnity, the Giants' first base coach, quickly sized up the situation and ran onto the field, wrestling the ball away from Evers and throwing it into the stands. In any case, Evers did touch second base with a ball in his glove, if not the ball that was in play, and appealed to umpire O'Day for a ruling. Actually the Giants' fate had been sealed in Pittsburgh several weeks before when, with O'Day in charge, Evers had made an appeal on the identical play and had been turned down. In the meantime, O'Day had realized that Evers was correct, and, although the rule was commonly ignored, he called Merkle out. The game was declared a one-to-one tie because by then it was too dark to continue play. Controversy over the decision reached a fever pitch when the Giants dropped all five of their remaining games, ended the season in a tie with the Cubs, and lost a replay of the suspended contest for the title. The fans heaped scorn on poor Merkle (although, to his credit, Manager John McGraw supported him) and raised the outraged cry "we was robbed." Even such a famous umpire as Bill Klem called O'Day's ruling "the rottenest decision in the history of baseball." But the Giants' "winning run" could have been invalidated for several reasons—in particular, because McGinnity interfered with a ball in play—and, on balance, O'Day's decision was just and courageous.

Photographer, Francis P. Burke

National League umpires William Hart and Ernest Quigley (left), Conkey (above left) and Cy Rigler (above right), the man who began the custom of raising his right hand to signify a called strike. The life of an umpire has never been easy—subjected to verbal abuse by players and fans, he is expected to remain calm at all times, although Rigler once punched Bill Dahlen, the manager of the Dodgers, because he protested a call too violently. The pay was poor and so were the working conditions. Umpires were given dressing rooms only after the turn of the century at the insistence of Bill Klem, who claimed that it was embarrassing to ride back to the hotel in uniform, especially if the home team had lost. But, as the famous Tim Hurst is supposed to have said to his grousing colleague Silk O'Loughlin, "You can't beat them hours."

The packed grandstand of West Side Park—the home of the Chicago Cubs until 1916, when they abandoned this ramshackle structure and moved into a new brick and steel stadium.

Photographer, Francis P. Burke

Photographer, Francis P. Burke

Handsome Christy Mathewson of the Giants was the greatest right-handed pitcher in the history of the National League with the possible exception of Grover Cleveland Alexander, the man who tied Matty for most lifetime wins in the senior circuit at 373. Mathewson had speed, pinpoint control (in 1913 he pitched 68 consecutive innings without giving up a base on balls), and his famous fadeaway pitch—a screwball or reverse curve that broke down and away from left-handed batters. Matty was an artist on the mound with a perfect memory of hitters' weaknesses—it was said that he never made a pitching mistake more than once. His record could have been even more spectacular if he had possessed a mean streak, but his image of clean living and fair play made him the most popular player of the era and an idol to the nation's youth.

Photographer, Francis P. Burke

Photographer, W.M. Van der Weyde

Shortstop Joe Tinker (far left and left) and second baseman Johnny Evers (posing above at first base) were two-thirds of the Cubs fine double play combination, immortalized in Franklin P. Adams's verse "Tinker to Evers to Chance." While this "trio of Bear cubs . . . fleeter than birds" did make many a Giant "hit into a double," it is doubtful that they were without peer in their day—they just had the best publicity.

Photographer, Francis P. Burke

Photographer, Francis P. Burke

On the far left Evers demonstrates his follow-through, while on the left Frank Chance shows how he leaps for a high throw. Tinker, Evers, and Chance were elected to the Hall of Fame as a unit in 1946.

Prince Hal Chase was the finest fielding first baseman in the game, but his fame as a gloveman was counterbalanced by his infamous career as a crooked ballplayer. Chase bet freely on games, often against his own team, and on such occasions it was natural and easy for Prince Hal to influence the outcome. He also tried, sometimes successfully, to induce other players to throw games, and he was eventually blacklisted from organized baseball.

Photographer, Francis P. Burke

Southpaw Rube Marquard starred for the Giants and then for the Brooklyn Dodgers. In 1912, he broke Tim Keefe's record of 19 consecutive wins by taking 20 straight. For years Marquard has been credited only with tying Keefe's mark, but by modern scoring rules one of the games he pitched in that stretch should have been a victory for Rube, even though it was given to Jeff Tesreau—he relieved Tesreau in the top of the ninth, the opposition went ahead by one run, and then the Giants scored two runs in the bottom of the frame to win.

Photographer, Francis P. Burke

Johnny Kling (above) was a stalwart catcher for the Chicago Cubs from 1900 to 1910, except for the 1909 season, which he sat out in a futile bid for higher pay. Doc Crandall (lower right) was an effective moundsman for several seasons with McGraw's Giants, and Big Ed Walsh (upper right) of the Chicago White Sox was the greatest of all spitball artists—he still holds the record for the lowest lifetime earned run average at 1.82.

Photographer, Francis P. Burke

Photographer, Francis P. Burke

Photographer, Francis P. Burke

95

Photographer, Francis P. Burke

Photographer, Francis P. Burke

Napoleon "Larry" Lajoie (upper left) may not have been the game's greatest second baseman, but he was undoubtedly the most graceful man ever to play the position. A superb hitter during his glory years with Cleveland, Lajoie became one of the sport's most popular figures. When he served as Cleveland's manager for several seasons, the team was named the Naps in his honor. Red Ames (lower left) was another sound arm on the Giant pitching staff. Here he warms up under the watchful eye of John McGraw. Germany Schaefer (above), the second baseman on Detroit's pennant-winning clubs in 1907 and 1908, was another natural eccentric in the Rube Waddell mold. Once, when he was on first and another Tiger runner was on third, he tried to work the double steal, drawing a throw at second so the man on third could score. The catcher, however, let Schaefer advance unmolested, so on the next pitch Germany turned around and ran back to first, hoping to draw a throw this time. Although the backstop was too stunned to do anything, Schaefer had, in effect, accomplished the impossible—stealing first base.

Photographer, Francis P. Burke

Photographer, Francis P. Burke

Doc White was the left-handed ace of the Chicago White Sox for many years, putting together seven straight winning seasons between 1904 and 1911. He was the complete-game victor in the deciding contest of the 1906 World Series in which the underdog White Sox (known as the Hitless Wonders because their team batting average that year was .230) took their northside rivals, the Cubs, four games to two. In addition to his pitching career, White dabbled in music, collaborating with his friend Ring Lardner on several tunes.

Photographer, Francis P. Burke

In this series of photos, Doc White illustrates the stages of a pitcher's motion—windup, pitch, and follow-through.

Photographer, Francis P. Burke

3

The Hustling Years

According to many an older fan, the years from 1910 to 1920 were baseball's classic era, the period when the game was played the way it should be played. There is much to be said for that point of view. Walter Johnson and Grover Cleveland Alexander—two men who could reasonably claim to be baseball's greatest pitchers—were in their prime, averaging 26 wins per season, and the great Christy Mathewson was still dazzling hitters well into the decade. These were also the years of peak performance for the game's greatest center fielder (Tris Speaker), second baseman (Eddie Collins), and all-around offensive threat (Ty Cobb). Cobb's composite batting average from 1910 to 1919 was an astounding .386, and he led both leagues in hitting every one of those years except 1916, when Speaker edged him out.

But the claim of classic status rests on more than the presence of individual stars. Since its inception, baseball had sought a balance between offense and defense, but in the decade 1900-1910 the scales were heavily weighted on the defensive side. Pitchers dominated the sport with trick deliveries like the spitball, the shine ball, and the emery ball. In 1908, the composite earned run average for all pitchers in the National League was 2.34—a mark low enough to lead the league in best *individual* earned run average in many recent seasons. In 1911, however, the offense was given a necessary boost with the introduction of the cork-center baseball. The dead-ball era was over, and now when a batter met a pitch squarely it flew a reasonable distance at a reasonable rate instead of plopping into an infielder's glove. Also, new baseballs began to be used with greater frequency—no longer could a pitcher husband a rough, darkened sphere inning after inning until the batter could hardly distinguish the object he was supposed to hit.

But even with the livelier ball, baseball was by no means the slugging spectacle it was to become. Home runs were still at a premium (in most years of the decade

fewer home runs were hit by an entire league than were belted out by the 1961 New York Yankees), and such inside-baseball tactics as the stolen base and the hit-and-run were polished to perfection (the 1911 New York Giants were the deftest base thieves of the modern era, stealing successfully 347 times—as many bases as are stolen today by *all* the National League teams in a season). Additional strategic refinements that became popular in this era were the use of pinch hitters and relief pitchers and the granting of an intentional walk in order to create a force play. Each of these developments was decried by some fans and players as the potential ruin of baseball, but the trend toward specialization seems to be inevitable. One wonders how these doomsayers would react to today's Oakland Athletics, who employ men whose only function is to serve as pinch runners.

The owners prospered in this decade, and no less than eight new stadiums were built between 1910 and 1916 to accommodate the rising number of fans (three of those ballparks—Chicago's Wrigley Field and Comiskey Park and Boston's Fenway Park—are still in use). It was this prosperity that led to an attempt in 1914 to establish another major league. The backers of the new Federal League, unlike the organizers of the Players League, had no desire to reform the game—they were solid capitalists who merely wanted a piece of the lucrative baseball pie. The Feds captured a number of established stars, and their venture gave the National and American League magnates some financial and legal headaches, but after the 1915 season they sold out to the established clubs. They had failed because of poor timing (the potential involvement of the United States in World War I cast a shadow of uncertainty over entertainment investments) and plain poor judgment (the pie just wasn't big enough to be cut three ways). The legacy of the Federal League, for the most part, was negligible. They built one handsome ballpark, which eventually became Wrigley Field, developed some good

Babe Ruth broke into the majors with the Boston Red Sox in 1914 as a 19-year-old left-handed pitcher. He was a very good one, too—setting a record for consecutive scoreless innings in World Series competition that stood until 1961.

Photographer, Francis P. Burke

new ballplayers like Edd Roush, and displayed a talent for christening their teams with ludicrous names—the Brooklyn Brookfeds and the Chicago Whales being the most notable examples.

When the United States finally entered World War I at the beginning of the 1917 season, the baseball world had no idea what to expect. There was no professional baseball at the time of the Civil War, and the Spanish-American War was a minor conflict that had hardly disturbed the game. Would the sport now be regarded as a mere frivolity and be told to close shop? Would ballplayers—a generally young and healthy group—be exempt from the draft? Would the fans still give the game their support? At first there was no interference from Washington, and the 1917 season went on as scheduled although a number of patriotic players enlisted (others, meanwhile, headed for the relative safety of war work in munitions factories and shipyards). In June of the following year, however, the government issued a "work or fight" order, which was designed to force draft-age men out of jobs that were not essential to the war effort. Exceptions were made for the major entertainment industries because they provided "necessary amusement," but no mention was made of baseball's status. When a delegation of club owners ventured to Washington and asked what they should do, they were told, almost as an afterthought, to end the 1918 season by September 1, and that year concluded with each team having played less than 130 games.

Baseball had survived the war with little damage, but in its aftermath the sport would come close to destruction. The Chicago White Sox of 1919 were one of the best squads in the history of the game, and they were heavily favored to beat Cincinnati in the World Series. When the Reds took them five games to three (the series was a best-five-out-of-nine affair that year), questions were immediately raised—not so much because of the

upset (such events had happened before) but because the games the Sox had lost were marked by a number of suspect plays. Seasoned observers had noticed these crucial miscues, but they were apparently unwilling to draw the logical conclusion, and it was not until the end of the 1920 season that the truth began to emerge. Eight Chicago players (the so-called Black Sox)—Swede Risberg, Ed Cicotte, Happy Felsch, Chick Gandil, Claude Williams, Fred McMullin, Joe Jackson, and Buck Weaver—had received as much as $15,000 apiece to throw the series, although some of them contended that they merely took the money and did nothing to influence the outcome. One wonders, for example, about Jackson, the hard-hitting left fielder who batted .375 in the series, but he testified before a grand jury that he did his best (or worst) to kick away the contests. And there is the case of Weaver, one of the slickest fielders ever to play third base, who received no money because the other conspirators claimed he didn't go along with the fix. There is no question, however, about star pitchers Cicotte and Williams, who threw as if they were in batting practice and made key "mistakes" in the field. The full story of the fix—who, if anyone, was the man behind it, and how many of the players really participated—has yet to be told, but the consequences were clear. Although none of the culprits was convicted in a court of law, each of them was barred from baseball for life. The sport's loose moral climate, which had tolerated betting on games by players, was replaced by a new sternness, and, above all, the scandal cast a pall of suspicion over the game (it should be noted that the Black Sox affair was not the first instance of a baseball fix, but only the boldest and most notorious attempt). The classic era of hustling baseball had ended with another kind of hustle—one that easily could have led to the decline of the game as the nation's chief spectator and participant sport. But, almost miraculously, the golden years of baseball were about to dawn.

The years from 1910 to 1920 were both satisfying and frustrating for John McGraw and his New York Giants. Little Napoleon led the club to four National League pennants, but each time they were defeated in the World Series. Perhaps the most painful blow of all was the 1912 loss to the Boston Red Sox—particularly because the Giants seemed to have the series in their collective back pocket. In the seventh and deciding game, the New York club went into the bottom of the tenth leading 2 to 1. When the first batter lifted an easy fly to center, Giant fans began to think that their jinx was broken, but Fred Snodgrass dropped the ball. Although Snodgrass redeemed himself on the next play by making a spectacular catch of Harry Hooper's long drive, Christy Mathewson, the man of impeccable control, proceeded to walk the next batter, putting the winning run on base. Now came the key error, and, strangely enough, it involved first baseman Fred Merkle, whose failure to touch second had cost the Giants a pennant in 1908. Boston's next hitter, Tris Speaker, lifted a little foul pop-up in Merkle's direction, but Fred stood on first as though hypnotized while the Giant's slow-footed catcher chased the ball and just missed it. Knowledgeable baseball men have contended that here was a case in which Merkle was the real culprit, but Mathewson was probably more at fault since he called for the catcher to take the ball all the way. The shaken Giants seemed to know that they had given Boston one break too many, as Speaker singled, driving in the tying run. Then Gardner hit a sacrifice fly, the winning run scored, and the series was over. John McGraw's string of post-season futility would end only in the 1920s when the Giants took three world titles in a row.

Photographer, Francis P. Burke

A movie sequence of Ruth's batting stroke shows that every ounce of his 6′ 2″, 215-pound frame is behind the ball at the moment of contact.

The Babe at 16 (when he was just George Herman Ruth) in the uniform of Baltimore's St. Marys Industrial School. Ruth was committed to the institution as a juvenile delinquent when authorities discovered that he was living in his father's saloon.

The reaction of major league baseball to the First World War was a mixture of avarice and comedy. Voices were raised in some quarters suggesting that such a frivolous activity as baseball had no place in wartime, but the club owners hardly shared these sentiments and lobbied vigorously for business as usual. For the most part, the owners had their way, and the war's effect on baseball was not especially severe, even though the 1918 season was shortened to 130 games. In an attempt to show that the sport was helping to make the world safe for democracy, both major leagues had their teams conduct military drill, with the players carrying bats instead of rifles. Here the Chicago White Sox do their best to impersonate the Coldstream Guards. Needless to say, the White Sox didn't win the $500 prize that American League President Ban Johnson offered to the best-drilled squad.

Photographer, Francis P. Burke

108

By 1912, Nick Altrock (left) and Germany Schaefer were both members of the Washington Senators. Altrock would remain with Washington as a coach long after his playing days were over, teaming up with Al Schacht to provide the fans with comic relief before games and between innings. At the end of the 1933 season, he was inserted into the lineup as a pinch-hitter by manager Joe Cronin, and thus, at the age of 57, he became the oldest man ever to participate in a major league game.

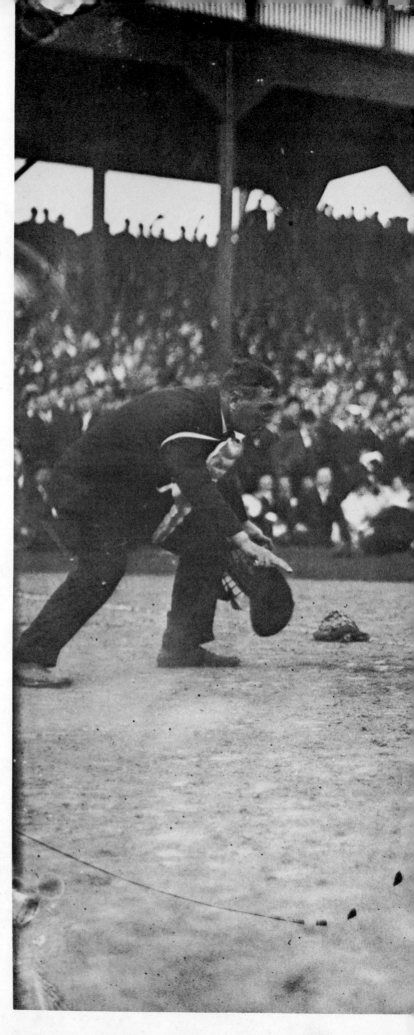

A run crosses the plate in exciting fashion during a contest between the Chicago Cubs and the Pittsburgh Pirates. The Cubs by this time had moved from their old West Side Park to the handsome facility constructed for the Chicago Whales, the Windy City's entry in the short-lived Federal League. Renamed Wrigley Field, the stadium is still the Cubs' home.

Photographer, Francis P. Burke

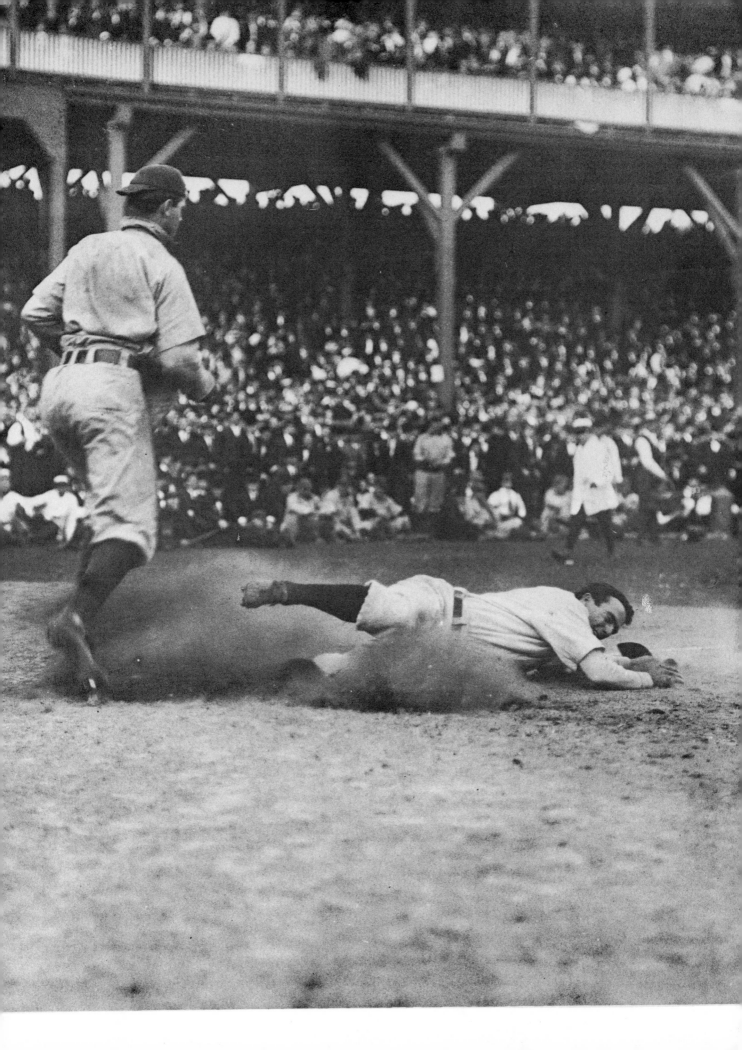

The fourth-place Chicago White Sox of 1912 were an undistinguished crew except for Big Ed Walsh who pitched his last 20-win season that year.

Photographer, Francis P. Burke

114

The 1912 New York Giants took the National League crown by ten games over Pittsburgh. The Giants were a running club, and their team total of 319 stolen bases is the third highest in modern major league history.

Photographer, Francis P. Burke

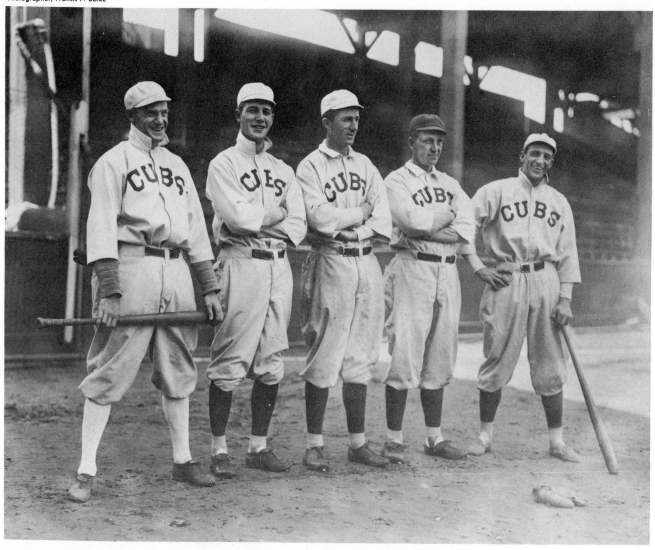

The outfielders (above) and the catchers (right) of the 1913 Chicago Cubs. The backstops (left to right) are Jimmy Archer, Mike Hechinger, Roger Bresnahan, and Tom Needham. According to his contemporaries, Archer had the strongest and most accurate throwing arm ever seen behind the plate. Bresnahan, in the twilight of his career, had just come to the Cubs after four years as the player-manager of the St. Louis Cardinals.

Photographer, Francis P. Burke

Walter Johnson, the Big Train, spent his entire 21-year career pitching for the Washington Senators, and his magnificent record is all the more remarkable considering that Washington was a weak team during most of that period. As his nickname implies, Johnson was as fast as any man who ever threw, and he holds the lifetime records for strikeouts and shutouts. His total of 416 victories is second only to Cy Young's, and virtually every man who faced Johnson has said that he was the greatest pitcher of all time.

Photographer, Francis P. Burke

118

Rogers Hornsby, the premier right-handed hitter in the history of the National League, made a scientific study of batting technique and holds the second-highest lifetime batting average at .358. In 1924, he hit .424—the highest single-season mark of the modern era—and he won the National League batting title six seasons in a row. Hornsby broke in with the St. Louis Cardinals as a shortstop in 1915, and, although a fine fielder, he didn't settle down to one position until 1920 when he made second base his home.

Photographer, Francis P. Burke

Old teammates Christy Mathewson (left) and Roger Bresnahan, now manager of the Cubs, chat before a game in 1915. Matty was then in the midst of his first poor season with the Giants since his rookie year, and in the middle of the 1916 campaign, John McGraw would ship him to Cincinnati as a player-manager.

Photographer, Francis P. Burke

Christy Mathewson was not notably successful in his three years as a manager in Cincinnati, finishing seventh once and fourth twice. There are very few instances in baseball history of ex-pitchers making good field leaders, and the same holds true for great players in general, so perhaps Matty had two strikes against him from the start.

Photographer, Francis P. Burke

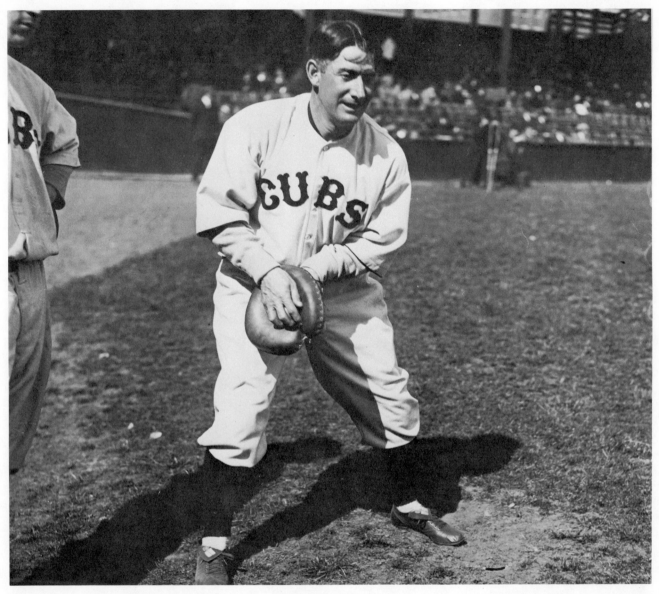

Roger Bresnahan, one of the wiliest catchers in the game and the Giants' backstop from 1903 to 1908, was one of the few very fast men ever to play a position noted as a refuge for the slow afoot. Although he was credited with the invention of shin guards, those essential pieces of protective equipment had been around for some time—Bresnahan was just the first man to wear them on the outside of his uniform instead of hiding them under his socks.

Photographer, Francis P. Burke

Grover Cleveland Alexander, like Walter Johnson, was a superb pitcher who labored for many years with an inferior team—in his case, the Philadelphia Phillies. In addition to this handicap, Old Pete's home park during those years, Baker Bowl, had the closest right field fence in the majors. Despite these problems and a pronounced taste for strong drink, Alexander was the dominant pitcher in the National League after Mathewson slacked off, and his career win total of 373 tied Matty for the most victories by a National League moundsman. Alexander also holds the record for most shutouts in a single season at 16, and he broke into the majors with the most successful rookie year a pitcher ever had—28 and 13 in 1911.

The 1915 Detroit Tigers (above) led the league in batting and runs scored, but they were edged out for the top spot in a hard-fought pennant race, finishing only 2½ games behind the Boston Red Sox. Ty Cobb (in the back row, fifth from the left) led the league with a .367 batting average and stole 96 bases, a record that stood until 1962. The Chicago White Sox that year (right) finished third, but they were a team on the rise who would take the pennant in two years after just missing out in 1916.

Photographer, Francis P. Burke

Photographer, Francis P. Burke

The 1915 St. Louis Cardinals (above) were led by Miller Huggins, the feisty little man who would manage the Yankees to six pennants in the Babe Ruth era, but even his touch couldn't turn the Cards into winners and they finished sixth. Baseball's best squad in 1915 was the Boston Red Sox (right) who beat the Phillies in the World Series, four games to one. Back row (left to right): Del Gainor, first base; Dutch Leonard, pitcher; Duffy Lewis, outfield; Cody; Vean Gregg, pitcher; Bill Carrigan, manager-catcher; Ernie Shore, pitcher; Ray Collins, pitcher; Tris Speaker, outfield; Babe Ruth, pitcher. Middle row: Larry Gardner, third base; Rube Foster, pitcher; Smokey Joe Wood, pitcher; Pinch Thomas, catcher; Dick Hoblitzel, first base; Harry Hooper, outfield; Heinie Wagner, second base. Front row: Jack Barry, infield; Hal Janvrin, infield; Carl Mays, pitcher; Hendriksen; William; Glennon; Everett Scott, shortstop; Herb Pennock, pitcher. Boston's outfield of Hooper, Speaker, and Lewis often is named as the finest defensive unit ever assembled.

Photographer, Francis P. Burke

128

Photographer, Francis P. Burke

129

Photographer, Francis P. Burke

Two National League champions who lost in the World Series—(left) the 1918 Cubs (defeated by the Red Sox) and (below) the 1917 Giants (victimized by the White Sox). The Giants' demise featured another one of those odd plays that plagued the club in post-season competition. In the fourth inning of the final game, Eddie Collins of the Sox was on third when the batter hit sharply back to pitcher Rube Benton, leaving Collins caught off base. But Benton failed to execute the rundown play properly, throwing to third baseman Heinie Zimmerman instead of to the catcher, and when Collins slipped past the backstop, there was nothing Heinie could do but chase the fleet runner across the plate. Although Zimmerman looked like the goat of the play, it was hardly his fault. As he said when questioned by reporters—"What was I supposed to do with the ball? Throw it to the umpire?"

Big Ed Reulbach (right) and Bill Lathrop (far right) both pitched for Chicago clubs, but there the resemblance ends. Reulbach was a mainstay for the Cubs, leading the league in winning percentage for three straight years, while Lathrop had only one victory in two seasons with the White Sox. Reulbach, a Notre Dame graduate, was one of the few college men in the early days of the game, and he once accomplished the remarkable feat of pitching two shutouts in one day.

Photographer, Francis P. Burke   Photographer, Francis P. Burke

A close play at the plate, as the Cincinnati Reds meet the
Chicago Cubs in 1915.

Photographer, Francis P. Burke

Charley Hall (above and right) of the Boston Red Sox, one of baseball's first relief specialists, demonstrates his windup and follow-through in Chicago's Comiskey Park.

Photographer, Francis P. Burke

Photographer, Francis P. Burke

Zack Wheat, who spent all but one of his 19 years in the majors as the Brooklyn Dodgers' left fielder, was a pleasure to watch at bat or in the field. A line-drive hitter with a .317 lifetime batting average, Wheat is remembered best for his strong, accurate arm and his ability to race into left center and turn sure doubles and triples into outs. On the left he happily demonstrates his throwing form, and on the right he warms up before a game (note the catcher biting off a chunk of chewing tobacco—the ballplayer's pacifier).

Photographer, Francis P. Burke

Smokey Joe Wood was a man who triumphed over adversity. In 1912, at the age of 22, the hard-throwing Boston Red Sox right-hander experienced what is probably the greatest single season a pitcher ever had—he won 34 games (including 16 straight), lost only 5, and took 3 out of 4 from the Giants in the World Series. But the next season his arm went bad, and by 1916 Wood was out of baseball. Smokey Joe had always been a good hitter, however, and he convinced his old roommate Tris Speaker, now with Cleveland, to give him a trial as an outfielder. By 1918 he was a regular for the Indians, and he played good ball for four more seasons, retiring in 1922 to become the baseball coach at Yale, where he served for two decades.

Photographer, Francis P. Burke

Stanley Coveleski, a young man from the Pennsylvania coal fields, was preceded to the majors by his brother Harry, who became known as "The Giant Killer" when he beat the New York club three times in one week at the end of the 1908 season (this was just after the Merkle incident, and if the Giants had won any of those games they still would have claimed the pennant). Stanley had a trial with the Philadelphia Athletics in 1912, and made it for good with Cleveland in 1916. In the minors he had transformed himself from a good pitcher into a great one by acquiring and perfecting the spitball—a pitch he learned to control better than almost anyone else (once he hurled seven innings of a game without throwing a single pitch outside the strike zone).

Photographer, Francis P. Burke

Third baseman Heinie Zimmerman, posing here in a seemingly awkward spread stance, was a powerful hitter for the Cubs and the Giants, leading the National League in 1912 with a .373 average. His career came to a sad end, however, in 1919 when he was an accomplice of Hal Chase in an incident that led to the banishment of both men from organized baseball. Benny Kauff of the Giants accused his two teammates of offering him a bribe to throw a game, and apparently there was hard evidence since John McGraw dropped Chase and Zimmerman from the team in the middle of a close pennant race. Oddly enough, Kauff himself was forced out of baseball in the following year by Commissioner Landis after he had been indicted for receiving stolen goods—a typically high-handed move on Landis's part, since a jury acquitted Kauff of the charge.

Photographer, Francis P. Burke

Connie Mack's $100,000 infield flanks outfielder Eddie
Murphy in this photograph taken before the fourth
game of the 1913 World Series. The players (left to
right) are Eddie Collins, second base; Jack Barry, shortstop; Murphy; Frank "Home Run" Baker, third base;
and John "Stuffy" McInnis, first base. This combination, the finest inner defense of the day, became a unit in
1911 and led the Athletics to three pennants in four
years. But after the 1914 World Series in which the
Athletics were swept by the Boston Braves, Mack
became disgusted with what he regarded as lackadaisical play, and he sold or traded most of his prize infield.
The 1915 Athletics responded by winning 43 games and
losing 109. Not until the mid-1920s would Philadelphia again become a contending team.

Photographer, Underwood & Underwood, New York

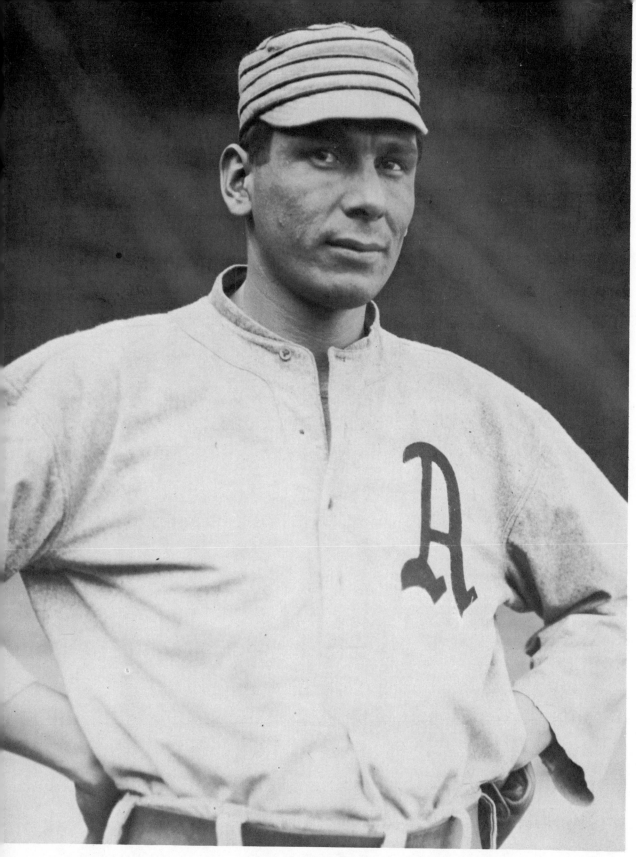

Charles Albert "Chief" Bender was one-quarter Chippewa (all ballplayers of American Indian ancestry seem to have been called "Chief"), a graduate of the Carlisle Indian School, and the man Connie Mack considered the best "money" pitcher on his staff. Bender was a key figure on each of the five pennant-winning squads the Athletics had between 1905 and 1914, but, like the $100,000 infield, he was gone after the 1914 World Series defeat.

In the twilight of his career, the 40-year-old Napoleon Lajoie became the Athletics' second baseman, replacing Eddie Collins, who had been sold to the White Sox. The move was ironic since Collins is considered the only man in the history of the American League ever to play the position better than Lajoie. Nap was the more graceful fielder, but Collins had an edge in speed, quickness, and range.

4

The Golden Years

It is no coincidence that the 1920s were baseball's golden years—it would have been odd, in fact, if they were not. An economic boom, unprecedented in scope and span, sent the nation's per capita income soaring; the population increased by 17 million; and people moved from rural to urban areas in ever-growing numbers. As a result, there were more potential fans than ever before who had more leisure time and more money to spend. The only things that might have prevented baseball from reaping this harvest were the moral blight of the Black Sox scandal and the competition of other sports and entertainment activities (the 1920s, after all, would be a golden era for boxing, tennis, golf, horse racing, and college football, not to mention the burgeoning motion picture industry). But baseball had an answer both to scandal and rival amusements—the unplanned and explosive advent of George Herman "Babe" Ruth.

In this day when a dozen "superstars" in as many sports are minted and marketed the year around, it is difficult to realize the impact Babe Ruth had on the national consciousness. First of all, he was something new. Home runs had been hit before, although in relatively modest numbers, but no one had made a specialty of thèm (when Ruth's initial season of slugging was over—he hit 29 homers for the Red Sox in 1919—considerable research had to be done before it could be determined whose record he had broken). Prior to the Babe, the home run was disparaged as much as it was celebrated—devotees of baseball strategy regarded it as a vulgar act of brute force—and before the construction of modern ballparks the typical round-tripper was merely a long drive that rolled between the outfielders and came to rest in the crowd. But there was no element of luck in a Ruthian blast—his drives not only went into the stands, they were prodigious blows that awed fans and players alike. Even his pop flies were spectacular feats that amounted to vertical home runs, and frequently he would be standing on second base by

the time the ball descended into a fielder's glove. It was this aura of the superhuman and the dramatic that made Ruth a national idol. His presence at the plate portended great events, and a Ruth strikeout was as exciting as another man's hit ("My God," the fans would say, "what if he'd connected with *that* swing?"). This is not to disparage his real achievements on the field, for Ruth, unlike many sluggers to come, was an all-around ballplayer who hit for a high average, fielded his position skillfully, and displayed an acute baseball sense. Ed Barrow, general manager of the Yankees, once said that he never saw the Babe make a mental mistake on the diamond.

Although there was no way for baseball to anticipate the arrival of Ruth, the sport was changed in significant ways once it became clear that the public responded to home-run baseball. The ball itself was made livelier when Australian wool, which could be more tightly wound, was substituted for the American variety—rueful pitchers would claim that if you held one of the new baseballs to your ear, you could hear its heart beating—and the moundsmen also suffered when one of their most effective weapons, the spitball, was banned in 1920. Although the development of the modern fielder's glove, with its deep pocket and leather webbing between the thumb and first finger, gave the defense some aid, the game during the golden era was based on explosive attack. Carefully honed strategies like the stolen base and the hit and run would still be used, but the big inning highlighted by one or more home runs was the order of the day.

The golden years also brought important changes in other areas. Judge Kenesaw Mountain Landis—a stern, opinionated jurist with a flair for publicity—became baseball's first commissioner, and he would hold the post until his death in 1944, ruling the sport with an iron (if sometimes erratic) hand. Together with Babe Ruth, Landis was responsible for restoring public

Everyone wanted to see the big game during baseball's golden era. Hoping to gain a vantage point, these fans are climbing a tree outside Chicago's Wrigley Field.

confidence in the game in the wake of the Black Sox scandal. Baseball's shaky status as an economic monopoly was strengthened in 1922 when the Supreme Court ruled in favor of organized baseball on an antitrust suit brought by the owners of the Baltimore entry in the old Federal League. The rationale of the decision, written by Justice Oliver Wendell Holmes, was that the business of baseball did not involve interstate commerce because "personal effort, not related to production, is not a subject of commerce." The baseball magnates breathed easily once again, and legal scholars, taking notice of baseball's large gate receipts, reflected that the law is capable of declaring an egg to be an orange.

The New York Yankees, led by Ruth and Lou Gehrig, were the dominant team of the era, but the rise of the St. Louis Cardinals, who won National League pennants in 1926 and 1928, was of greater long-range significance. The Cardinals had been one of baseball's poorest teams both competitively and financially when Branch Rickey joined their front office in 1919. Rickey saw a way for his economically disadvantaged franchise to compete with such wealthy squads as the New York Giants, who ensured their dominance by periodically purchasing the best players developed in the minor leagues. His plan was twofold—the Cardinals signed large numbers of inexperienced but promising young-sters to minor league contracts with the expectation that some would eventually become stars, and, to keep control over this garden of raw talent, the Cardinals began to purchase interests in minor league teams. The economic advantages of what came to be called the "farm system" were the small initial investment of capital (large bonuses for signing were unheard of in those days) and the avoidance of a heavy purchase price when a player became good enough to enter the majors. Although Rickey's methods were ridiculed at first, other teams scrambled to emulate them when they began to pay off, and today the success of a major league team depends for the most part on the strength of its farm system.

The golden years were literally a golden era for the club owners—with the exception of a few tailenders, every team in the majors made a profit during the decade. The fans who sent the turnstiles spinning followed the game with unprecedented interest; when clubs like Washington and St. Louis that had long been out of contention finally won pennants, those cities virtually came to a halt during the World Series as fans flocked to the ballpark or waited for up-to-date reports of the outcome. Baseball had worked the ultimate alchemy of transforming individuals into those strange beings called "rooters"—men and women whose basic identities seemed bound up with the teams that had captured their affections. Nowhere was this bond more intense than in the borough of Brooklyn. Dodger followers lived and died with their erratic stalwarts, and a mediocre season could be redeemed if enough victories were recorded over their hated rivals, the New York Giants. Giant fans, meanwhile, were not a shade less devoted to their champions, and perhaps such fusions of populace and team tell the story of the golden years better than anything else. Baseball was a sport and a business, but now it was also a kind of national religion that shaped America as much as America shaped it—a metaphor and a myth by which citizens interpreted their existence, playing out each summer the destinies charted in the off-season. The genteel game Alexander Cartwright formulated in 1845 had conquered the nation's consciousness.

Judge Kenesaw Mountain Landis of the Federal District Court for Northern Illinois was named baseball's first commissioner in an attempt to restore respectability to the sport at the time of the Black Sox scandal. Landis—an opinionated, publicity-seeking jurist whose flair for self-dramatization (apparent in these photographs) put him just this side of Judge Roy Bean—was in many ways the perfect man for the job. Baseball, above all, needed the appearance of sternness and incorruptibility, and Judge Landis had spent his career on the bench cultivating exactly that image. In legal circles, however, he was regarded as a judicial illiterate (a number of his Draconian decisions had been overturned) who ran his courtroom like an oriental potentate, and these traits would surface frequently during his career as commissioner.

These photographs of Ty Cobb posing with Judge Landis (left) and being introduced to the commissioner's young wife (above) are ironic, since one of Landis's most confused and capricious rulings involved the Detroit star. The public was startled after the 1926 season by the news that Cobb had been given his unconditional release and that Tris Speaker, Cleveland's player-manager, had resigned. Although both men were up in years they were still fine players, and Speaker had just led the Indians to a second-place finish. Eventually the story behind the affair leaked out of Landis's office—a former pitcher for Detroit, Dutch Leonard, had accused Cobb and Speaker of betting on a Detroit-Cleveland game in 1919, and Leonard had documented evidence to back up his charge. In addition, the implication was clear that the two stars had attempted to influence the outcome (Detroit, the team they bet on, did, in fact, win the contest). Landis's first impulse was to ban Cobb and Speaker for life, but public reaction, which the commissioner carefully watched, swung in the direction of leniency this time, and the Judge eventually reinstated both men just before the 1927 season.

The New York Yankees had played in the Polo Grounds (the Giants' home) since 1913 when they had to abandon ramshackle Hilltop Park, but in 1920 the Giants decided to shove their American League competitors out into the cold by refusing to renew the Yankees' lease. Brewery baron Jacob Ruppert, the Yankees' new owner, wangled a two-year extension from the Giants and began to build a magnificent structure that would seat 65,000 fans. Yankee Stadium was ready for the opening day of the 1923 season, and Babe Ruth christened his new playground by parking a three-run blast in the inviting right field stands.

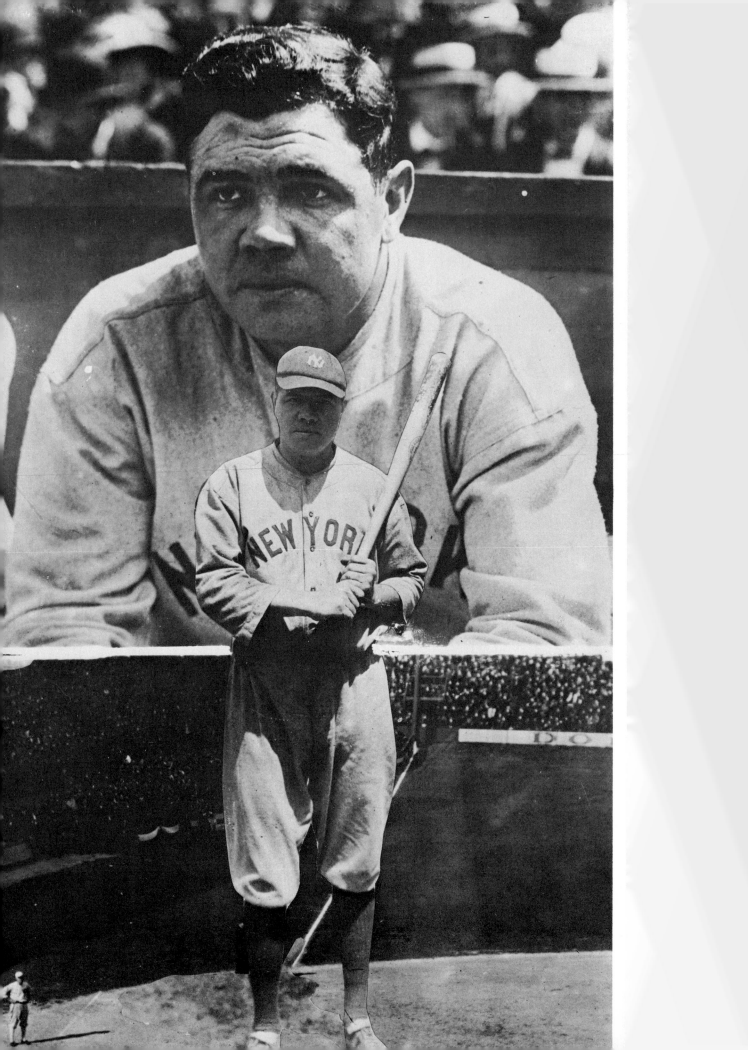

Babe Ruth's effect on baseball is almost impossible to describe. There had been famous players before him like Ty Cobb, and men such as Christy Mathewson and Napoleon Lajoie whose combination of skill and personality had endeared them to the fans, but Ruth was something else all together—a larger-than-life figure whose gargantuan feats and appetites, childish good-nature, and boyish hell-raising seemed to have been created to match the spirit of the Roaring Twenties. The Babe, of course, hit home runs, and undoubtedly this was one secret of his appeal, since any fan, no matter how unsophisticated, could appreciate the significance of a single mighty blow. But, above all, it was the way the man's achievements were highlighted by a natural, charismatic swagger that made him a national idol—it was even exciting to watch the Babe strike out.

Ruth shakes hands with Ed Barrow, a man who had a profound effect on his career. Although the move was probably suggested by right fielder Harry Hooper, it was Barrow who, as manager of the Red Sox, shifted Ruth to the outfield on the days he wasn't pitching. And when the Babe was sold to the Yankees after the 1919 season, Barrow soon followed him to New York as the club's general manager. There he engineered the trades that surrounded Ruth with a talented crew of athletes who would win seven pennants in the next fifteen years. Even if he had played for a weak team, Ruth would have been a popular figure, but as the star of these Barrow-assembled champions his skills were constantly in the limelight.

Ruth (left) in 1920—his first season with the Yankees and the year in which he burst onto the national scene by hitting 54 home runs (the previous record, which he had set the year before, was 29). In the 1926 series the Yankees were defeated by the St. Louis Cardinals in seven games, but the Babe (above) certainly wasn't at fault. He hit four home runs, including a series-record three in one game.

Photographer, Francis P. Burke

First baseman Lou Gehrig (right) followed Ruth in the Yankee batting order and was his principal rival as a slugger. Lou's 1931 total of 184 runs-batted-in is the highest in the history of the American League, and his record of 2,130 consecutive games (equivalent to slightly less than 14 seasons) will, undoubtedly, never be approached. In the photograph on page 163, Gehrig congratulates Ruth as the Babe sets the single-season home run record with his 60th roundtripper of 1927. Gehrig was second to Ruth in home runs that year, hitting 47. As some indication of the way these two men dominated the slugging statistics, consider these facts—the man who finished third behind Ruth and Gehrig had only 18 circuit blows, and the combined home run total of the two Yankees was almost twice as great as that of any other 1927 *team*.

Babe Ruth in 1920 (far left), 1928 (middle) and 1930 (left). Now that Ruth's single-season and career home run marks have been surpassed by, respectively, Roger Maris and Hank Aaron (who has also eclipsed the Babe's all-time runs-batted-in record), it is useful to remember that Ruth still holds the record for lifetime home run percentage, averaging 8.5 home runs for every 100 times he came to bat. No batter ever stepped to the plate who was more likely to hit one out than George Herman Ruth.

Although Tris Speaker, the great center fielder for Boston and Cleveland, never hit many home runs, no one in base-ball history had more doubles than Spoke's career total of 793. In the outfield he stationed himself just behind second base, gloving Texas Leaguers that would normally drop safely, and on deep drives he would turn his back to the plate, gauging the distance and direction of the blow more by sound than by sight, and pull down shots that he seemingly had no chance to reach. After the run-in that he and his friend Ty Cobb had with Judge Landis, he left Cleveland where he had spent eleven years, eight of them as player-manager, and finished his career with Washington and Philadelphia. Cobb (age 42) and Speaker (age 40) played their last season together as teammates in the Athletic outfield.

Photographer, Francis P. Burke

Another stalwart whose career ended at an advanced age was Honus Wagner. The 43-year-old Flying Dutchman appeared in less than half of Pittsburgh's games, most of them at first base, in the last of his 21 seasons, but he still hit .265.

A sparse crowd witnesses a close play at the plate, with the catcher attempting to apply a flying tag. Whatever call the umpire made, you can be sure he had an argument on his hands.

The Wrigley Field groundskeepers (above) prepare the park for the first game of the 1927 season (right). The Cubs would find themselves, 153 games later, in fourth place—the same spot they had occupied the year before.

Hope springs eternal in the spring of the year as the 1928 Cubs and their owner William Wrigley, Jr., prepare for the season in Scottsdale, Arizona. The Chicago White Stockings, ancestors of the Cubs, were the first team to head south for pre-season conditioning. In 1870 they traveled to New Orleans to avoid Chicago's cold winds.

172

8·Simmons   11·Grove   14·Summa   17·Bishop 20·H...
9·Cochrane 12·Earnshaw 15·Walberg 18·Boley   21·Ro...
10·Foxx   13·Dykes   16·Ehmke   19·Haas   22·Pe...

adelphia "Athletics"

1·John Shibe · Owners
2·Tom Shibe ·

3·Dr. E. V. Ebling · Trainer   5·Connie Mack · Manager
4·Wm. Gleason · Coach   6·Earl Mack · Coach
7·Eddie Collins · Captain

23·Quinn   26·Yerkes   29·Miller
24·Shores   27·Cronin   30·Burns
25·Breckinridge   28·French   31·Le Bourveau

COPYRIGHTED · 1929
BURKE & KORETKE
CHICAGO

The 1929 Philadelphia Athletics won the American League pennant, marking the end of Connie Mack's long climb back to the top after he had broken up his 1914 squad. Mack would follow virtually the same pattern again when his 1931 team failed in the World Series against the St. Louis Cardinals. Within a year or two, most of the Athletics' star players had been sold or traded, but this time there was no resurgence—Philadelphia remained near the bottom of the league for the rest of Connie's reign.

Photographer, Francis P. Burke

8·Hornsby 11·Grimm 14·McMillan 17·Malone
9·Wilson 12·Cuyler 15·Taylor 18·Carlson
10·Stephenson 13·English 16·Bush 19·Heathcote

icago "Cubs"

7·William Wrigley·Owner

1·Joe McCarthy·Manager
2·Wm. Veeck·President
3·J.O. Seys·Vice Pres.

4·Andrew Lotshaw·Trainer
5·Grover Land ⎫
6·James Burke ⎬ Coach

ir	23·Hartnett	26·Beck	29·Penner
ke	24·Root	27·Gonzales	30·Cvengros
son	25·Nehf	28·Moore	31·Schulte	32·Grampp

The National League Champion Chicago Cubs of 1929 broke a long drought for their fans (the team's last pennant had been in 1918), but they lost the series in five games to the Athletics. Even though the outcome was one-sided, the contests had more than their share of excitement. In the first game, the Athletics started 36-year-old Howard Ehmke, an apparently washed-up pitcher, who proceeded to strike out a World-Series-record thirteen men. In the fourth game, the Cubs were leading 8 to 0 and appeared to be well on their way to tying the series when the Athletics scored 10 runs in the seventh inning. And, in the final game, the Athletics, trailing 2 to 0, scored three runs in the bottom of the ninth to take it all.

Photographer, Francis P. Burke

The first game of the 1929 series finds every seat taken in Wrigley Field.

Everyone wanted to see the World Series, but everyone couldn't get into the park. On the left, Chicago patrolman Al Bibby catches young Joseph Weisbaum trying to scale the wall with a boost from Albert Berg. Fans who were too old to climb listened to the games on the radio.

Thousands of Chicago baseball fans gathered at the intersection of Madison and Market to watch the *Chicago Herald-Examiner*'s "Playograph" displaying the inning-by-inning results.

The Athletics' Jimmy Foxx crosses the plate with the first run of the 1929 series after driving a pitch from Charlie Root into the Wrigley Field stands.

On the left are Cubs' coach James Burke, center fielder Hack Wilson, and manager Joe McCarthy. Wilson hit .471 in the series, but he gave considerable impetus to the Athletics' ten-run outburst in the fourth game by losing several fly balls in the sun. At 5′ 6″ and 190 pounds, Wilson was hardly an ideal center fielder. Above are Cubs' Vice President J. O. Seyes and Joe McCarthy.

The manager of the 1929 Cubs, Joe McCarthy, flanked by his coaches, James Burke and Grover Land. The Cubs were Joe's first pennant-winning squad, but they were far from his last. In 1931 he took over the Yankees and led them to eight American League championships and seven world titles (including four in a row). Even though McCarthy had never played in the majors, he seemed to be a natural leader, and his calm yet firm approach was a key factor in the Yankees' success.

Photographer, Francis P. Burke

189

THE 1929 CHICAGO CUBS (pages 190-197)

Photographer, Francis P. Burke

Andrew Lotshaw, trainer

Joe McCarthy, manager

Grover Land, coach

William Wrigley Jr., owner

Rogers Hornsby, second base

James Burke, coach

Lewis "Hack" Wilson, outfield

Charlie Grimm, first base

Riggs Stephenson, outfield

Kiki Cuyler, outfield

192

Woody English, shortstop

Zack Taylor, catcher

Norm McMillan, third base

Guy Bush, pitcher

Pat Malone, pitcher

Cliff Heathcote, outfield

Hal Carlson, pitcher

Clarence "Footsie" Blair, infield

John "Sheriff" Blake, pitcher

Charles "Gabby" Hartnett, catcher, pinch hitter

Chester "Chick" Tolson, infield, pinch hitter

Charlie Root, pitcher

Art Nehf, pitcher

Mike Gonzalez, catcher

Clyde Beck, infield

Johnny Moore, outfield

Ken Penner, pitcher

John Schulte, catcher

Mike Cvengros, pitcher

Henry Grampp, pitcher

Tom Shibe, owner

THE 1929 PHILADELPHIA ATHLETICS

(pages 198-205)

Photographer, Francis P. Burke

John Shibe, owner

Dr. E.V. Ebling, trainer

198

Connie Mack, manager

Earl Mack, coach

William Gleason, coach

Eddie Collins, captain

Mickey Cochrane, catcher

Lefty Grove, pitcher

Jimmy Foxx, first base

George Earnshaw, pitcher

Jimmy Dykes, third base

Richard "Rube" Walberg, pitcher

Homer Summa, outfield, pinch hitter

Howard Ehmke, pitcher

Max Bishop, second base

George "Mule" Haas, outfield

Joe Boley, shortstop

Sammy Hale, infield

Ed Rommel, pitcher

Jack Quinn, pitcher

Cy Perkins, catcher

Bill Shores, pitcher

Bill Breckinridge, pitcher

Jim Cronin, infield

Carroll Yerkes, pitcher

Walt French, outfield

Edmund "Bing" Miller, outfield

Al Simmons, outfield

George Burns, infield

5

Backyards and Playgrounds

For the 600 athletes who play baseball in the major leagues each season, the game is not a game at all but a skilled profession, distinguishable from others mainly because one can practice it for only a brief span of time. And each season several thousand more young men in the minor leagues work toward a day of graduation that may never come. But behind these talented souls who give us our summer rations of vicarious pleasure there is another kind of baseball—a game more for participants than spectators, a game that is still a game.

Among the very young, baseball seems to break down into its component parts, which are assembled into a whole as the separate skills are mastered. First, perhaps, one simply tosses a ball in the air or bounces it off a wall, a barn, or a city stoop. A companion or two comes along, and now the game is catch or a variation of tag involving one or more runners and at least two basemen. Baseball's only other vital piece of equipment, the bat, is introduced, but hitting a thrown ball is not an easy task (the most difficult single act in sports, said Ted Williams), and some version of fungo hitting is adopted—the batter lifting flies to a group of fielders who accumulate points with successful catches until one of them has scored enough to take over at the plate. Gradually it becomes apparent that this is "just a kids' game" (on my block it was a talented tomboy who made that momentous decision), and we move on to a game where the batter faces an authentic pitcher. But it is still rare for two full teams to assemble, and we play one-o-cat, in which the players move up a position at a time and right field is Siberia.

And then real baseball finally comes, and the pleasures of team success are added to those of individual achievement. Sides are chosen, and, wonder of wonders, you aren't the last one picked—"He's okay," someone says, "he really hustles" (true or not, you certainly hustle that day). Inning after inning, images are stored in your mind—the day you face that big lefty who really throws smoke (and he's wild, too);

the line drive you catch in an act of pure self-preservation, shrugging it off with the nonchalance of an old pro; the clean single over the shortstop's head that drives in the tying run in the bottom of the ninth and the rush to complete that inning before the pitcher has to go home for dinner; the utter conviction that the best player in your neighborhood is as good as anyone anywhere and that it will be only a matter of time before he is starring in the majors; the resemblance no one else can see between the way you scoop up a grounder and the way Nellie Fox does it (of course, the wad in his cheek is chewing tobacco, not bubble gum); the melodic plonk of a bat dropped on schoolyard asphalt; the tube of mysterious neat's foot oil (what kind of an animal is a neat?) that you use to break in a new glove; the old man who stops to observe your game with a practiced eye (his "way to go" after a nice play is the equivalent of a standing ovation); and the day you yourself pause in your adult rounds at the sight of a well-used diamond and wait for the players to take the field:

Innings and afternoons. Fly lost in sunset.
*Throwing arm gone bad. There's your old ball game.**

A group of congressional pages choose sides in the traditional manner by walking hands up the bat. The boy with his hand at the top gets his first choice of players.

The only requirements for a game were enough players,
a bat, a ball, and a little open space.

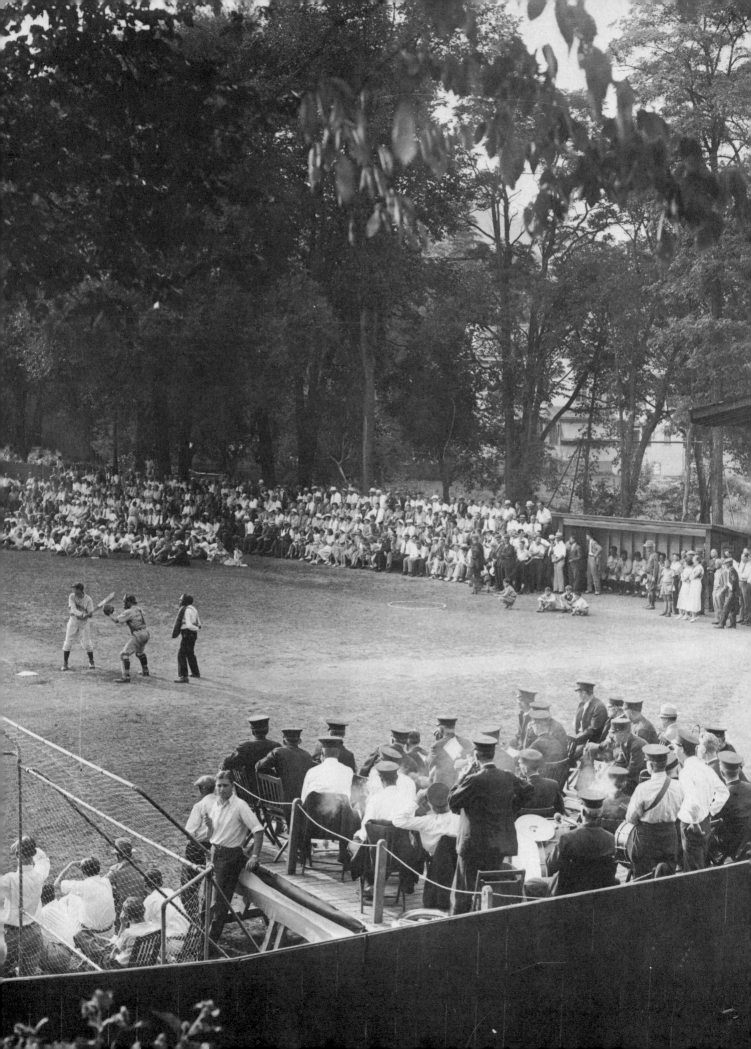

The opening game at Cooperstown's Doubleday Field
in 1934. The park attempts to recreate the atmosphere of
baseball's early days.

Photographer, Arthur J. Telfer; courtesy New York State
Historical Association, Cooperstown, New York

Frank Chance, the Chicago Cubs Hall of Fame first
baseman and manager, poses with potential Cleveland
Indian.

Two squads of orphans meet
in 1910 with the luxury of an
adult umpire. Was a long fly
to the swings a ground-rule
double?

Photographer, Arthur J. Telfer; courtesy New York State
Historical Association, Cooperstown, New York

215

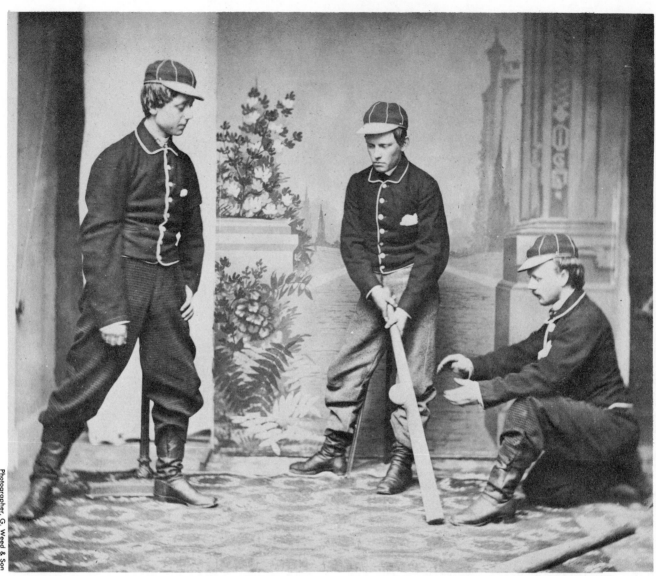

216

Will Chappel, pitcher; John A. Curtis, batter, and Will Crittenden, catcher of the Cazenovia, New York team (opposite page) posed for this photograph in 1865. The House of David team (above) was the most famous barnstorming squad in the country. The players all were supposed to be members of the House of David religious sect, but more often than not they were just fast, strong-armed lads who could grow beards. Such semi-pro clubs gave many a future major league star his first chance to play for pay—in their teens, and presumably before their voices changed, Smokey Joe Wood and Rogers Hornsby broke into pro ball with the Bloomer Girls.

Conhoy, Umpire,   Fitch, Mgr,   Alvah, Mascot,
Welch, l. f.   Ercanbrack, Carrier,   Wright, r. f,   Crane, c. f.
Gunnell, 3b.   L. Carr, s. s. (Capt.)   McElroy, 2b.   H. Carr, 1b.
Arnold, p.   Elger, c.   Folger, p.

MORAVIA BASE BALL CLUB = = SEASON OF 1899.
AMATEUR CHAMPIONS OF CENTRAL NEW YORK.

The Moravia, New York, Base Ball Club of 1899 took the amateur title of Central New York State.

The Laurens, New York, Base Ball Club, circa 1890.

The Cooperstown, New York, semi-pro team, circa 1888.

The 1885 Keokuk, Iowa, club of the Western League. Back row center is John Jackson, a talented second baseman who played under the name of Bud Fowler. Like most players of his race in that era he lived an itinerant existence, starring on integrated minor league teams or all-black semi-pro squads as the level of community prejudice dictated.

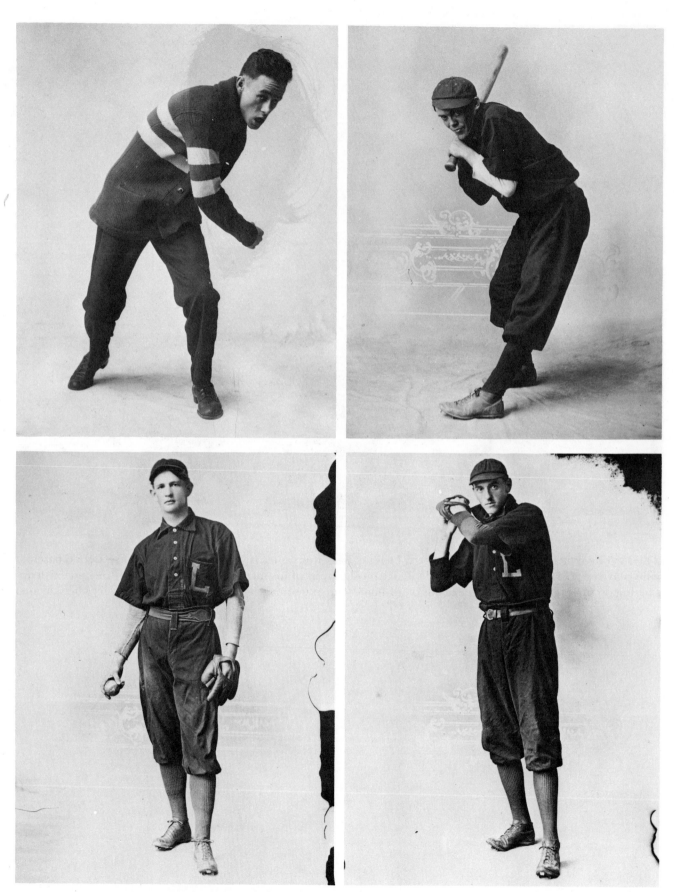

The players of the Leavenworth, Kansas, Hometown Team address the camera with varying degrees of seriousness.

Index